MRCP 1 'BEST OF FIVE'

KEY TOPICS SUMMARIES

3rd Edition

W Stephen Waring
BMedSci MB BCh BAO MRCP (UK)
Lecturer in Clinical Pharmacology,
Scottish Poisons Information Bureau
Royal Infirmary of Edinburgh
Edinburgh

Paul O'Neill
BSc (Hons) MB ChB MD FRCP (London)
Honorary Consultant Physician
Professor of Medical Education
University of Manchester
Manchester

PASTEST
Dedicated to your success

© 2004 PASTEST LTD
Egerton Court
Parkgate Estate
Knutsford
Cheshire
WA16 8DX

Telephone: 01565 752000

First published 1987
Second edition 1997
Third edition 2004

ISBN 1 904627 05 6

A catalogue record for this book is available from the British Library.

The information contained within this book was obtained by the author from reliable sources. However, while every effort has been made to ensure its accuracy, no responsibilty for loss, damage or injury occasioned to any person acting or refraining from action as a result of information contained herein can be accepted by the publishers or authors.

PasTest Revision Books and Intensive Courses

PasTest has been established in the field of postgraduate medical education since 1972, providing revision books and intensive study courses for doctors preparing for their professional examinations.

Books and courses are available for the following specialties:
MRCGP, MRCP Parts 1 and 2, MRCPCH Parts 1 and 2, MRCPsych, MRCS, MRCOG Parts 1 and 2, DRCOG, DCH, FRCA, PLAB Parts 1 and 2.

For further details contact:

PasTest, Freepost, Knutsford, Cheshire WA16 7BR
Tel: 01565 752000   Fax: 01565 650264
www.pastest.co.uk   enquiries@pastest.co.uk

Typeset by Breeze Ltd, Manchester.
Printed and bound by MPG Ltd, Bodmin, Cornwall

CONTENTS

CONTRIBUTORS

Dr Shani Esmail
BSc(Hons) MB BChir MRCP (UK)
Research Fellow in Clinical Pharmacology
University of Edinburgh
Western General Hospital
Edinburgh

Dr Peter Aquino
MB BCh BAO MSc MPhil
Research Fellow in Epidemiology
Newham Primary Care Trust
Plaistow Hospital
London

INTRODUCTION

The MRCP Part 1 examination consists of two papers each lasting three hours. Both papers contain 100 'Best of Five' questions (one answer is chosen from five options). The exam is composed of a fixed number of questions drawn from different specialties, which are randomly distributed between both papers. Further details of the exam format are available from www.mrcpuk.org/mrcppt. **A positive marking scheme is used, so that no marks are deducted for a wrong answer.**

One-best answer/'Best of Five' MCQs

The format of the MRCP Part 1 exam has evolved over a number of years. The purpose of the exam is to test the candidate's ability to apply knowledge and problem-solving skills in the context of a clinical scenario, rather than simply be able to recall isolated facts.

Each 'one-best' MCQ has a question stem, which usually contains clinical information, followed by five branches. All five branches are typically homologous (eg all diagnoses, all laboratory investigations, all antibiotics, etc) and should be set out in a logical order (eg alphabetical). Candidates are asked to select the ONE branch that is the best answer to the question. A response is not required to the other four branches. The answer sheet is, therefore, slightly different to that used for true/false MCQs.

A good strategy that can be used with many well-written one-best MCQs is to try to reach the correct answer without first scrutinising the five options. If you can then find the answer you have reached in the option list, then you are probably correct.

Application of Knowledge and Clinical Problem-Solving

A true/false MCQ format had been used in earlier MRCP Part 1 exams, which had been used to test recall of a broad range of factual knowledge. However, the current one-best-answer format is better at testing application of knowledge and problem-solving skills. It is rare that questions included in the exam will have only one possible answer. Most questions will present two or three plausible answers to the stem. Therefore, candidates are assessed on their ability to select the 'best' and most appropriate answer. In order to answer these questions correctly, candidates must apply basic knowledge – not just be able to remember it. Unlike the previous true/false MCQ format, there is a much lower chance of randomly guessing the correct stem (20%).

To get the best value from this book you should commit yourself to an answer for each item before you check the correct answer. It is only by being sure of your own responses that you can ascertain which questions you would find difficult in the examination. For each question, an explanation has been provided for why the answer is preferred over the suggested alternatives. However, given the constraints imposed by space, candidates are advised to refer to larger reference texts for more detailed study, for example PasTest's *Essential Revision Notes for MRCP, Revised Edition*, by P Kalra will provide you with essential notes on all aspects of the syllabus.

NORMAL VALUES

Haematology

Haemoglobin	
Males	13.5–17.5 g/dl
Females	11.5–15.5 g/dl
MCV	76–98 fl
PCV	35–55%
WCC	4–11 × 10^9/l
Neut.	2.5–7.58 × 10^9/l
Lymph.	1.5–3.5 × 10^9/l
Plt	150–400 × 10^9/l
ESR	0–10 mm in the 1st hour
PT	10.6–14.9 s
PTT	23.0–35.0 s
TT	10.5–15.5 s
Fib	125–300 mg/dl
I. Vitamin B_{12}	160–900 pmol/l
Folate	1.5–10.0 mg/l
Ferritin	
Males	20–250 mg/l
Females	10–120 mg/l

Immunoglobulins

IgM	0.5–2.0 g/l
IgG	5–16 g/l
IgA	1.0–4.0 g/l

Biochemistry

Na^+	135–145 mmol/l
K^+	3.5–5.0 mmol/l
Urea	2.5–6.5 mmol/l
Cr	50–120 μmol/l
ALT	5–30 U/l
AST	10–40 U/l
Bili.	2–17 μmol/l
Alk P	30–130 U/l
Alb.	35–55 g/l
gGT	5–30 U/l
aFP	< 10 ku/l
CCa^{2+}	2.20–2.60 mmol/l
PO_4^{2-}	0.70–1.40 mmol/l
CK	23–175 U/l

LDH	100–190 U/l
Amylase	< 200 U/l
Lactate	0.5–2.2 mmol/l
Mg^{2+}	0.75–1.00 mmol/l
Urate	0.1–0.4 mol/l
CRP	0–10 mg/l

Diabetes

Glucose	
Random	3.5–5.5 mmol/l*
Fasting	< 7 mmol/l
HbA_{1c}	< 7.0%

Endocrinology

TSH	0.17–3.2 mU/l
fT_4	11–22 pmol/l
fT_3	3.5–5 pmol/l
Cortisol	
0900	140–500 nmol/l
2400	50–300 nmol/l
Growth hormone	< 10 ng/ml
Cholesterol	< 5.2 mmol/l
Triglycerides	0–1.5 mmol/l
LDL	< 3.5 mmol/l
HDL	> 1.0 mmol/l
Total/HDL	< 5.0
FSH	1–25 U/l
LH	1–70 U/l
Prolactin	< 400 mU/l

Blood Gases

pH	7.35–7.45
$Paco_2$	4.6–6.0 kPa
Pao_2	10.5–13.5 kPa
HCO_3^-	24–30 mmol/l
BE	−2–2.0 mmol/l

CSF

Protein	< 0.45 g/l
Glucose	2.5–3.9 mmol/l (two-thirds plasma)
Cells	< 5 (WCC)
Opening pressure	6–20 cmH$_2$O

* If > 5.5 then OGTT 2 hrs:	7–11.1 = IGT
	> 11.1 = DM

QUESTIONS

CARDIOLOGY

There are usually 15 cardiovascular (vascular disease) questions in the exam. In the core section, the examiners still tend to emphasize clinical cardiology, common physical signs and pharmacology. Most exams will contain questions such as 'the causes of a loud first heart sound include' or 'a third heart sound is found in'. You should start your revision by making a list of these and summarising the key features of each. Clinical science topics that you might consider include:

- Causes of giant *a* waves in the JVP
- Causes of cannon waves
- Loud S1
- Reversed, wide fixed, and variable splitting of S2
- Causes of S3, S4
- Anatomy of the coronary arteries
- Valsalva manoeuvre
- Valvular stenosis and incompetence – explanations of clinical signs
- Common congenital heart diseases (often a core topic)
- Causes of a prolonged QT interval
- ACE inhibitors (frequent question, could be considered as a pharmacology topic)
- Constrictive pericarditis (haemodynamic consequences).

1   **A 65-year-old man regularly attends the Cardiology
         Outpatient Clinic. He reports increasing shortness of breath
         on exertion, reduced appetite and dusky skin discoloration.
         Investigations show normal full blood count, Na^+
         135 mmol/l, K^+ 4.1 mmol/l, urea 8.0 mmol/l, creatinine
         100 μmol/l, aspartate transaminase (AST) 160 U/l, alkaline
         phosphatase (ALP) 180 U/l, albumin 39 g/l, bilirubin
         48 μmol/l, free T_4 24 pmol/l and thyroid-stimulating hormone
         (TSH) 0.2 mU/l. An echocardiogram showed an enlarged left
         atrium and apparently normal left ventricular function, and
         pulmonary function tests showed a restrictive lung defect
         and reduced CO transfer. Which of the following provides the
         best explanation for this patient's presentation?**

☐   A   Amiodarone toxicity
☐   B   Bacterial pneumonia
☐   C   Congestive heart failure
☐   D   Haemochromatosis
☐   E   Hyperthyroidism

2   **A 47-year-old man is admitted to the Emergency Department
         with chest discomfort and palpitations. An electrocardiogram
         (ECG) shows broad cardiac complexes (around 0.15 ms) with
         a ventricular rate of 186 beats per minute. Which of the
         following findings would most strongly suggest a
         supraventricular rather than a ventricular origin of the
         arrhythmia?**

☐   A   The absence of P waves
☐   B   The appearance of 'fusion beats'
☐   C   The presence of 'capture beats'
☐   D   Variable S1 morphology
☐   E   Ventricular concordance

3   **You are called to review an ECG taken from a 66-year-old
         man, who is a patient in the Coronary Care Unit (CCU),
         because the QT interval is reported as 0.560 ms. Which one
         of the following factors would be most likely to have been
         responsible for QT-interval prolongation in this patient?**

☐   A   Amiodarone
☐   B   Erythromycin
☐   C   Hyperkalaemia
☐   D   Ischaemic heart disease
☐   E   Sotalol

4   A 76-year-old man is noted to have regular 'cannon waves' in his jugular venous pressure waveform. Which of the following underlying cardiac abnormalities is most likely to be responsible?

☐ A   Complete heart block
☐ B   Nodal or junctional rhythm
☐ C   Tricuspid regurgitation
☐ D   Ventricular extrasystoles
☐ E   Ventricular tachycardia

5   A 58-year-old man was recently admitted with severe central chest pain. An ECG showed ST elevation across the anterior leads, and a diagnosis of acute myocardial infarction was established. He is now pain-free and you are reviewing his medication prior to discharge home. Which of the following would be least likely to reduce his risk of a future myocardial infarct?

☐ A   Aspirin
☐ B   Atenolol
☐ C   Atorvastatin
☐ D   Isosorbide mononitrate
☐ E   Lisinopril

6   You see a 72-year-old woman in the Cardiology Outpatient Clinic. She has established congestive heart failure with an ejection fraction of 35%. Which of the following treatments would be expected to achieve the greatest reduction in future cardiovascular mortality?

☐ A   Atenolol
☐ B   Digoxin
☐ C   Furosemide
☐ D   Spironolactone
☐ E   Valsartan

7   You are asked to review a 45-year-old man attending a
             cardiovascular risk clinic. He is found to have: fasting
             triglyceride 1.8 mmol/l, total cholesterol 9.6 mmol/l, and
             high density lipoprotein (HDL) cholesterol 0.9 mmol/l. You
             decide to commence treatment with simvastatin. Which of
             the following best describes its therapeutic effects?

☐   A   It will reduce coronary risk irrespective of the cholesterol reduction
         achieved
☐   B   Low density lipoprotein (LDL) cholesterol will not fall unless dietary
         cholesterol is also restricted
☐   C   Simvastatin raises liver transaminase activity
☐   D   Statins lower LDL cholesterol and triglyceride concentrations
☐   E   Statins lower LDL cholesterol and HDL cholesterol concentrations

8   A 45-year-old man attends the Emergency Department with a
             four-week history of fatigue, breathlessness and fever. On
             examination he is found to have peripheral oedema, raised
             jugular venous pressure with giant V-waves, and
             hepatomegaly. You arrange admission for further
             investigations. Which of the following best explains the
             presenting features?

☐   A   Alcohol-related cardiomyopathy
☐   B   Bacterial endocarditis
☐   C   Pulmonary hypertension
☐   D   Pulmonary stenosis
☐   E   Sarcoidosis with cardiac involvement

9   A local GP has performed an ECG on an otherwise well 64-
             year-old man as part of a 'well man' health screen. The
             appearance is not considered normal and the ECG has been
             forwarded for your opinion. You find that the R wave in V1 is
             strikingly prominent, such that the overall QRS complex is
             positive. Which of the following might best explain this ECG
             appearance?

☐   A   Anterior myocardial infarction
☐   B   Dextrocardia
☐   C   Hypothyroidism
☐   D   Left ventricular hypertrophy
☐   E   Right bundle branch block

10 **A 18-year-old woman presents to the Emergency Department with a history of sudden-onset palpitations.** An ECG initially showed a narrow-complex tachycardia with a heart rate of 154 beats per minute, and this spontaneously reverted to sinus rhythm with a heart rate of 78 beats per minute. Which of the following would most strongly suggest the need for urgent investigation of an underlying cause?

- ☐ A Oral contraceptive pill use
- ☐ B Prolonged PR interval
- ☐ C Slurred upstroke of the QRS complex
- ☐ D Strong family history of thyroid disease
- ☐ E T-wave inversion in lead V1

11 **During a CCU ward round, you review a patient who has been admitted for investigation of chest pain. On examination you note the presence of a third heart sound. Which one of the following statements most accurately describes the clinical significance of this sign?**

- ☐ A It indicates stiffening of the left ventricular myocardium
- ☐ B It is a recognised complication of hypothyroidism
- ☐ C It is a recognised sign of severe mitral incompetence
- ☐ D It characteristically indicates underlying myocardial pathology
- ☐ E It is a characteristic finding in atrial fibrillation

12 **A 35-year-old woman, who is taking the oral contraceptive pill, is referred to the Cardiology Outpatient Clinic by her GP for investigation of intermittent chest pain and breathlessness. The clinical history is strongly suggestive of recurrent pulmonary thromboembolic disease. Which one of the following findings would suggest the possibility of an alternative diagnosis?**

- ☐ A A loud pulmonary component of the second heart sound
- ☐ B An early diastolic murmur at the left sternal edge (LSE)
- ☐ C Clinical history of haemoptysis
- ☐ D Cyanosis
- ☐ E Widespread bifid P waves on the ECG

13   **A 58-year-old man presents to the Cardiology Outpatient
            Clinic with progressive breathlessness on exertion and ankle
            swelling. You consider the possibility of underlying alcoholic
            cardiomyopathy. Which of the following features would most
            strongly support this diagnosis?**

☐   A   Abnormal liver biochemistry
☐   B   Clinical signs of chronic liver disease
☐   C   ECG indicating sinus rhythm
☐   D   Echocardiography suggestive of restrictive cardiomyopathy
☐   E   History of binge-pattern alcohol consumption

14   **A patient has been referred for investigation of a systolic
            murmur, consistent with that of aortic stenosis. Which of the
            following clinical features is most suggestive of severe valve
            stenosis?**

☐   A   Loud aortic component of the second heart sound
☐   B   Loud murmur of 5/6 intensity
☐   C   Narrow pulse pressure
☐   D   Presence of a third heart sound
☐   E   Slow-rising character of the carotid pulse

15   **A 19-year-old man is referred to the Medical Outpatient Clinic
            for investigation of intermittent syncope, palpitations and
            dizziness. His older brother died suddenly at the age of 30.
            On examination you find a harsh systolic murmur and you
            suspect an underlying diagnosis of idiopathic hypertrophic
            cardiomyopathy. Which of the following clinical findings
            would most strongly support this possibility?**

☐   A   30-mmHg systolic pressure difference between left and right arms
☐   B   A decrescendo murmur at the left lower sternal margin during early
        diastole
☐   C   A slow-rising carotid pulse
☐   D   Double apical impulse
☐   E   Increased murmur intensity during squatting

16   **A 38-year-old woman presents with palpitations and
            breathlessness, and is found to have atrial fibrillation. A
            transthoracic echocardiogram suggests the possibility of an
            underlying ostium secundum atrial septal defect (ASD).
            Which of the following features would most strongly support
            this diagnosis?**

☐   A   Harsh late systolic murmur
☐   B   Left bundle branch block
☐   C   Oligaemic lung fields on chest X-ray
☐   D   Right axis deviation on the ECG
☐   E   Wide fixed splitting of the first heart sound

17 An 11-month-old child is referred to the Cardiology Clinic with a queried diagnosis of Tetralogy of Fallot. Which of the following features would not be consistent with this diagnosis?

- [ ] A A history of central cyanosis
- [ ] B A history of syncope
- [ ] C An ejection systolic murmur over the pulmonary area
- [ ] D A loud pulmonary component of the second heart sound
- [ ] E A right ventricular heave

18 A 26-year-old woman is referred to the Cardiovascular Risk Clinic for assessment of persistent hypertension. On examination, you note that she is of small stature and that an ejection systolic murmur is audible over the aortic area, and there is significant radio-femoral delay. Which of the following diagnoses would best explain these clinical features?

- [ ] A Coarctation of the aorta
- [ ] B Patent ductus arteriosus
- [ ] C Phaeochromocytoma
- [ ] D Primary hyperaldosteronism
- [ ] E Significant renovascular disease

19 A 45-year-old Asian woman presents with leg swelling, increasing abdominal girth and shortness of breath. She has been previously well, apart from a previous medical history of tuberculosis (TB). On examination, her jugular venous pressure (JVP) is elevated and rises with inspiration. There are prominent x and y descents. You think she may have constrictive pericarditis. Which one of the following is not a recognised feature of constrictive pericarditis?

- [ ] A Pericardial calcification on chest X-ray
- [ ] B Myocardial thickening on echo
- [ ] C Non-pulsatile hepatomegaly
- [ ] D Equalisation of end-diastolic pressures in all four chambers on cardiac catheterisation
- [ ] E Pericardial knock in diastole

20 You review a 55-year-old man in the Cardiology Outpatient Clinic. He has persisting atrial fibrillation despite attempted DC cardioversion and you decide to commence digoxin treatment. Which of the following statements most accurately describes the effects of this drug?

- [ ] A It acts predominantly at the sinoatrial node
- [ ] B It improves cardiovascular morbidity and mortality
- [ ] C It increases stroke volume and cardiac output
- [ ] D It is a positive chronotrope
- [ ] E It lessens the frequency of paroxysmal atrial fibrillation

CLINICAL PHARMACOLOGY

There are a total of 20 questions on Clinical Pharmacology and Toxicology, randomly distributed between both papers. Generally, candidates are intimidated by this topic because of the breadth of knowledge examined. However, a number of specific topics are frequently examined. These include:

* Poisoning – you cannot cover all the possible things that people take. You have to concentrate on the common ones. These include salicylates, paracetamol, tricyclic antidepressants and lithium. Frequently, the College asks questions that cover more that one drug, such as those related to antidotes or dialysis
* Drug interactions appear in most papers, frequently related to anticoagulants, digoxin, hypoglycaemics, amiodarone and anti-epileptics.
* Each of these drugs is an important topic in its own right and you must spend time revising them. Other topics include sulfasalazine and thiazides.
* You should consider alterations in pharmacokinetics – prescribing in renal failure, first-pass effect.
* Questions on drugs and pregnancy are frequently included, such as teratogenic effects and contraindications in breastfeeding.
* You should cover systems-based pharmacology when you are revising that particular organ system. Examples would be drugs and the kidney (interstitial nephritis) or the lung (pulmonary fibrosis).
* It is also worth revising a little about drugs and the skin (for example, photosensitivity).
* Remember, when answering questions about drugs, it is safer to say that something does occur, rather than being confident that it does not.

21　　A 65-year-old woman with established hypertension is regularly reviewed in the Cardiovascular Risk Outpatient Clinic. She is complaining of dizziness and fatigue. Her resting pulse rate is 62 beats per minute, seated blood pressure (BP) 148/82 mmHg, and erect BP 112/78 mmHg. You consider that her symptoms are attributable to postural hypotension. Which of the following drugs is most likely to be responsible?

☐　A　Atenolol
☐　B　Bendroflumethiazide
☐　C　Lisinopril
☐　D　Moxonidine
☐　E　Nifedipine

22　　A 68-year-old man with persistent atrial fibrillation has been taking warfarin 3–4 mg/day for nine months. His international normalised ratio (INR) has usually been maintained at 2.0–2.5 but, during a routine check, was found to be 6.8, and his GP contacts you for advice. The patient has recently received a number of additional treatments. Which of the following would be most likely to cause a significant increase in his INR?

☐　A　Aspirin
☐　B　Diclofenac
☐　C　Erythromycin
☐　D　Omeprazole
☐　E　Phenytoin

23　　A 22-year-old female medical student has suffered two grand mal seizures within three months. She is taking the combined oral contraceptive pill and wishes to continue this. No precipitating factors for the seizures are identified, and a diagnosis of primary generalised epilepsy is made. Which of the following would be the most appropriate first-line treatment?

☐　A　Carbamazepine
☐　B　Ethosuximide
☐　C　Lamotrigine
☐　D　Lorazepam
☐　E　Phenytoin

24 **A 49-year-old man attends the Medical Outpatient Department eight weeks after a myocardial infarction.** His current medications are aspirin 75 mg daily and atenolol 100 mg daily, and he describes a moderate exercise capacity free of symptoms. You note that his total serum cholesterol is 5.9 mmol/l and triglycerides 2.8 mmol/l. Which of the following options would be the most appropriate in this situation?

☐ A Bezafibrate 200 mg tid
☐ B Dietary advice and re-check lipids in six weeks
☐ C Discontinue β-blocker and re-check lipids in six weeks
☐ D Simvastatin 20 mg nocte
☐ E Simvastatin 20 mg nocte AND bezafibrate 200 mg tid

25 **A 17-year-old girl is admitted to the Emergency Department with a suspected intentional paracetamol overdose, and the plasma concentration was 248 mg/l four hours post-ingestion. Which of the following features would most strongly suggest an additional drug overdose or toxin ingestion?**

☐ A Abdominal tenderness
☐ B Hypoglycaemia
☐ C Hypotension
☐ D Metabolic acidosis
☐ E Respiratory depression

26 **Pharmacovigilance plays a crucial role in ensuring the safety of medications administered across wide populations. Which of the following statements is most accurate in relation to the Yellow Card reporting system?**

☐ A Adverse effects delayed more than two weeks should not be reported
☐ B Adverse events due to unlicensed medication use should not be reported
☐ C Adverse events should not be reported if the causal link is uncertain
☐ D Around 75% of all serious adverse events are reported
☐ E All adverse events for newer drugs should be reported

27 **A 56-year-old woman presents with nausea and vague abdominal discomfort. She is found to be jaundiced, and liver biochemistry shows: alanine aminotransferase (ALT) 38 U/l, ALP 249 U/l, bilirubin 56 μmol/l and albumin 39 μg/l. Which of the following drugs is most likely to account for these abnormalities?**

☐ A Paracetamol
☐ B Oxytetracycline
☐ C Rifampicin
☐ D Omeprazole
☐ E Co-amoxiclav

28   A 45-year-old woman has been receiving lithium carbonate
      for a number of years for bipolar depression. She complains
      of progressive fatigue and generalised weakness. She is
      found to have a pulse rate of 66 beats per minute, BP
      132/78 mmHg, and the following biochemical findings: Na⁺
      151 mmol/l, K⁺ 3.4 mmol/l, urea 13.2 mmol/l, creatinine
      186 μmol/l, calcium 2.5 mmol/l, albumin 38 g/l, and lithium
      1.8 mmol/l. Which is the most likely underlying cause of
      these findings?

□ A Drug-induced glomerulonephritis
□ B Hypothyroidism
□ C Lithium toxicity
□ D Multiple myeloma
□ E Nephrogenic diabetes insipidus

29   A 48-year-old man presents to the Emergency Department
      with sudden onset of severe upper abdominal pain and
      vomiting. He has had high blood pressure for three years,
      treated with bendroflumethiazide 2.5 mg daily and atenolol
      100 mg daily. He is found to have a rash over the extensor
      aspects of both arms. An ECG shows a heart rate of 104 beats
      per minute, but is otherwise normal. Which of the following
      is the most likely underlying diagnosis?

□ A Acute myocardial infarction
□ B Acute pancreatitis
□ C Thoracic aortic dissection
□ D Acute hepatitis
□ E Gastroenteritis

30   A 22-year-old man is brought to the Emergency Department
      after being found unconscious in university lodgings. The
      ambulance crew found several ibuprofen tablets by his side.
      On examination, his respiratory rate is 22 breaths per
      minute, heart rate 128 beats per minute, BP 104/60 mmHg,
      pupil size and responses are normal, reflexes are normal and
      symmetrical, and plantar responses are extensor.
      Investigations show: Na⁺ 144 mmol/l, K⁺ 4.6 mmol/l,
      bicarbonate 7 mmol/l, urea 6.0 mmol/l and glucose
      9.0 mmol/l. Which of the following is the most likely
      diagnosis?

□ A Paracetamol toxicity
□ B Benzodiazepine overdose
□ C Methanol toxicity
□ D Opiate overdose
□ E Tricyclic antidepressant overdose

31   You are reviewing the medications of a patient attending the
      Renal Outpatient Clinic. Which of the following factors is the
      most important to consider when adjusting prescribed drug
      doses in renal failure?

☐ A   Aqueous solubility of the drug
☐ B   Estimated creatinine clearance
☐ C   Height and weight of the patient
☐ D   Serum creatinine concentration
☐ E   The underlying aetiology of the renal impairment

32   A 56-year-old woman is referred to the General Medical
      Outpatient Department with a three-month history of
      palpitations. She describes a good exercise tolerance and no
      other symptoms, and there is no significant past medical
      history. The GP letter includes an ECG that shows atrial
      fibrillation with a ventricular rate of 96 beats per minute. She
      is currently receiving digoxin 250 µg daily. On examination
      she is found to have an irregular pulse with a rate of 84
      beats per minute and BP 138/76 mmHg. Physical
      examination is otherwise normal. Which of the following
      treatments would be most appropriate as additional
      treatment?

☐ A   Amiodarone
☐ B   Aspirin
☐ C   Aspirin plus dipyridamole
☐ D   Warfarin
☐ E   Warfarin plus aspirin

33   A 42-year-old woman presents to the Emergency Department
      with reduced conscious level and slurred speech. She has
      long-standing schizophrenia and depression. Her current
      medications are chlorpromazine, fluoxetine and diazepam.
      She is found to have generally diminished reflexes and
      absent plantar responses, but cranial and peripheral
      neurological examination is otherwise normal. Plain chest X-
      ray and resting ECG are normal. Investigations show: Na^+
      129 mmol/l, K^+ 3.8 mmol/l, urea 8.6 mmol/l, creatinine
      78 µmol/l, glucose 8.1 mmol/l and normal liver biochemistry.
      Which of the following is the most likely cause of the
      hyponatraemia?

☐ A   Chlorpromazine
☐ B   Diazepam
☐ C   Fluoxetine
☐ D   Psychogenic polydipsia
☐ E   Syndrome of inappropriate antidiuretic hormone (ADH) secretion

34   **A 57-year-old man with rheumatic heart disease is an**
           inpatient in the General Medicine Department and is receiving
           regular intravenous gentamicin and co-amoxiclav for
           suspected infective endocarditis. Which of the following is
           true of gentamicin monitoring?

☐ A Dose interval should be determined by the trough level
☐ B Dose should be reduced if the trough level is high but peak level
       satisfactory
☐ C Nephrotoxicity is not a recognised complication if peak and trough
       levels are satisfactory
☐ D Nephrotoxicity risk is increased by concurrent furosemide treatment
☐ E Peak levels should normally be kept between 15 and 25 µg/ml

35   **A pharmaceutical company representative presents data on a**
           new cholesterol-lowering drug. The data indicate that in
           healthy volunteers and patients with hypercholesterolaemia
           the drug is more potent than any other agent currently
           available, and it is to be marketed at the same price as
           existing treatments. Which of the following is true?

☐ A Further studies are required to determine the safety of the drug
☐ B The new drug should be initiated in preference to existing
       treatments
☐ C The new drug should be substituted in patients receiving existing
       treatments
☐ D The new drug will achieve greater cholesterol reductions than other
       treatments
☐ E The new drug will cause a greater reduction in cardiovascular risk

36   **You see a 32-year-old woman with rheumatoid arthritis who**
           is taking regular ibuprofen for pain in her wrists. Which of
           the following is true regarding non-steroidal anti-
           inflammatory drugs (NSAIDs)?

☐ A Adverse effects occur in around 5% of patients
☐ B NSAIDs reduce the relapse rate of rheumatoid arthritis
☐ C Therapeutic and adverse effects are mediated by lipo-oxygenase
       inhibition
☐ D They are implicated in around half of cases of gastric ulceration
☐ E They enhance the antihypertensive effect of β-blockers

37   **In developing a new antibiotic drug, phase 1 clinical trials have shown the drug has bioavailability of 1–12% after oral administration in healthy subjects. Which of the following statements is true?**

- [ ] A   Is unlikely to have significant adverse effects
- [ ] B   It is likely to have high aqueous solubility
- [ ] C   Its absorption might increase up to tenfold if taken with food
- [ ] D   The drug is unlikely to be clinically useful
- [ ] E   The oral dose will need to be high to ensure adequate plasma concentrations

38   **You are asked in confidence for some advice by a 24-year-old staff nurse on your ward. She has recently been commenced on phenytoin for idiopathic generalised epilepsy and is concerned about the potential long-term adverse effects of the treatment. Which of the following is the most commonly recognised complication of phenytoin?**

- [ ] A   Atrial fibrillation
- [ ] B   Hair loss
- [ ] C   Osteoporosis
- [ ] D   Slurred speech
- [ ] E   Thrombocytopenia

39   **A 42-year-old married woman with long-standing atrial fibrillation and Graves' disease attends the Outpatient Department for review. She is receiving regular digoxin 125 μg daily and warfarin 2–3 mg daily. Pulse rate is irregular at 76 beats per minute, BP 134/68 mmHg and she is clinically euthyroid. She explains that she is hoping to become pregnant and asks what to do about her medications. Which is the most appropriate advice regarding her anticoagulation?**

- [ ] A   Aspirin should be substituted during the first trimester
- [ ] B   Low molecular weight heparin should be substituted during the first trimester
- [ ] C   Low molecular weight heparin should be substituted for the duration of the pregnancy
- [ ] D   Anticoagulation should be discontinued for the duration of the pregnancy
- [ ] E   Should continue anticoagulation because risks of discontinuing outweigh potential benefit

40   **A 22-year-old woman taking the combined oral contraceptive pill asks for your advice. She has read a recent magazine article which suggested that there are important side effects of this treatment. Which of the following is true?**

☐ A   Combined preparations should be avoided in sickle cell disease
☐ B   Combined preparations may cause malignant melanoma to progress more rapidly
☐ C   Previous venous thromboembolism is a contraindication to treatment
☐ D   Progesterone-only preparations are preferred in epilepsy
☐ E   Progesterone-only preparations increase blood pressure

41   **Which of the following drugs should be used with particular caution in elderly patients?**

☐ A   Amoxicillin
☐ B   Beclometasone
☐ C   Bumetanide
☐ D   Nifedipine
☐ E   Omeprazole

42   **A 30-year-old man with a history of depression and personality disorder is normally taking amitriptyline 75 mg bd and diazepam 10 mg nocte. He presents to the Emergency Department following a deliberate overdose of around 30 diazepam tablets two hours earlier. He is drowsy and poorly cooperative with the clinical examination. Cardiorespiratory findings are satisfactory. Which of the following is true regarding diazepam?**

☐ A   Blood levels are useful for identifying patients likely to require ventilation
☐ B   The half-life of its sedative effects is around two to three hours
☐ C   It is only active after metabolic activation in the liver (a pro-drug)
☐ D   It is water-soluble and predominantly cleared by renal excretion
☐ E   The sedative effects are exaggerated by alcohol

43   **You are asked to review a 45-year-old man who has returned to the ward following a lymph node biopsy procedure. He has been complaining of persisting nausea and has vomited four times. You decide to prescribe an anti-emetic treatment. Which of the following statements regarding anti-emetic therapy is correct?**

☐ A   Cyclizine is preferred to metoclopramide for nausea after recent myocardial infarction (MI)
☐ B   Domperidone acts by blockade of central dopamine receptors
☐ C   Metoclopramide acts through peripheral cholinergic receptor blockade
☐ D   Metoclopramide is a recognised cause of drug-induced parkinsonism
☐ E   Ondansetron is only effective in treating nausea associated with chemotherapy

44   **A 32-year-old woman attends the Emergency Department with increasing pain and redness of her left breast, which has progressively worsened over the past five days. She is breastfeeding her three-month-old son after an uneventful pregnancy and delivery, and there is no significant past medical history. On examination, her temperature is 38.5 °C and there is marked erythema and tenderness overlying the lateral aspect of her left breast, associated with tenderness on axillary node palpation. You diagnose cellulitis and wish to commence oral antibiotic treatment. Which of the following would be the most appropriate therapy?**

☐ A   Amoxicillin
☐ B   Erythromycin
☐ C   Metronidazole
☐ D   Trimethoprim
☐ E   Vancomycin

45   **A new drug is being developed for treatment of type 2
diabetes. Preclinical tests show that it is metabolised almost
exclusively by hepatic acetylation. In considering the design
of future clinical trials of the drug, which of the following
factors is correct?**

☐   A   Adverse effects are more likely in slow acetylators
☐   B   It is likely to be less effective in slow acetylators
☐   C   Its pharmacological effects should be studied in slow-and-rapid
          acetylator populations
☐   D   Typically, more than 85% of patients with type 2 diabetes are slow
          acetylators
☐   E   Typically, more than 85% of Eskimos are slow acetylators

RESPIRATORY MEDICINE

There are usually 15 questions in the exam on respiratory medicine randomised across both papers. Frequently, these are based on pulmonary physiology. Unlike cardiology, it is unusual to have any question on physical signs. Common topics that you should cover include:

- Increased and decreased transfer factor
- Hypoxia
- Hypercapnoea, hypocarbia (hyperventilation)
- Acid–base disturbance (could be considered under metabolic medicine – a very important topic)
- Normal pulmonary physiology (you have to understand this to answer many questions on deranged physiology)
- Oxygen dissociation curve and shifts
- Respiratory failure (combination of above topics)
- Physiological effects of long-term oxygen therapy
- Pathological effects (and clinical symptoms, signs, aetiology) of sleep apnoea syndrome.

46   Mr Smith, a 30-year-old man with α_1-antitrypsin (α_1-AT) deficiency, attends the Respiratory Clinic for review. Which of the following statements regarding this condition is correct?

- ☐ A   Increased risk of colonic carcinoma is a recognised feature
- ☐ B   Prenatal diagnosis is not yet available
- ☐ C   Patients who manifest disease usually have the PiZZ genotype
- ☐ D   Smoking cessation makes little impact on prognosis
- ☐ E   Serum α_1-antitrypsin levels are usually elevated at diagnosis

47   Mr Smith, an obese 58-year-old man, presents to his GP complaining of daytime somnolence and poor concentration. His wife says that he snores a lot at night, and sometimes stops breathing for a few moments. He is referred to the Respiratory Outpatient Department and you consider the diagnosis of obstructive sleep apnoea. Which of the following statements regarding this condition is correct?

- ☐ A   Daytime sleepiness can usefully be assessed using the APACHE scoring system
- ☐ B   Diagnosis is based on posterior fossa MRI scan appearances
- ☐ C   Nocturnal continuous positive airway pressure (CPAP) has been shown to be ineffective in the majority of cases
- ☐ D   Pulmonary hypertension is a commonly recognised feature
- ☐ E   Type I respiratory failure is a commonly recognised feature

48 You see a 67-year-old man with chronic obstructive pulmonary disease (COPD) in the Respiratory Outpatient Department. He has been reading about long-term oxygen therapy on the Internet and wants to ask you a few more questions about it. Which of the following statements regarding domiciliary oxygen treatment is correct?

- ☐ A Between six and ten hours' treatment daily is sufficient for most patients
- ☐ B It has no impact on the progression of pulmonary hypertension
- ☐ C Domiciliary oxygen treatment is associated with increased risk of viral pneumonitis
- ☐ D There is no impact on patient survival
- ☐ E Treatment is based on arterial gas analyses measured when the patient is clinically stable on at least two occasions, three weeks apart

49 A 37-year-old woman presents with a six-month history of progressive breathlessness. Pulmonary function tests show diminished carbon monoxide (CO) transfer factor. Which of the following diagnoses is the most likely underlying cause?

- ☐ A Exercise
- ☐ B Ventricular septal defect with left-to-right shunt
- ☐ C Polycythaemia
- ☐ D Pulmonary embolus
- ☐ E Pulmonary haemorrhage

50 The haemoglobin-oxygen dissociation curve is an important determinant of tissue oxygen delivery for any given Pao_2. Which one of the following factors is known to displace the dissociation curve to the left, such that haemoglobin is less efficient at delivery of oxygen to tissues?

- ☐ A Chronic hypoxia due to cyanotic heart disease
- ☐ B Increased lactate production
- ☐ C Increased $Paco_2$
- ☐ D Increased serum pH
- ☐ E Increased temperature

51 A 46-year-old man is admitted to the Emergency Department and found to have a low pulse oximetry recording (86%). Arterial blood gas analysis finds: pH 7.38, Pao_2 7.8 kPa, and $Paco_2$ 6.8 kPa. Which of the following possible diagnoses offers the best explanation for these findings?

- ☐ A Acute asthma
- ☐ B Diazepam overdose
- ☐ C Pulmonary embolism
- ☐ D Pulmonary haemorrhage
- ☐ E Pneumothorax

52   **A 47-year-old non-smoking woman has been referred to the Respiratory Clinic with a two-week history of cough and haemoptysis. Which of the following is the most likely underlying cause?**

☐ A   Bacterial pneumonia
☐ B   Bronchial adenoma
☐ C   Mesothelioma
☐ D   Pulmonary hypertension
☐ E   Sarcoidosis

53   **A 35-year-old lady presents with a 12-day history of haemoptysis and a 24-hour history of haematuria. In the last 24 hours she has become increasingly breathless and oliguric. Investigations show: Na$^+$ 136 mmol/l, K$^+$ 6.5 mmol/l, bicarbonate 14 mmol/l, creatinine 960 μmol/l, haemoglobin 9.8 g/dl. Chest X-ray shows patchy interstitial infiltration, predominantly affecting both lower zones. Which of the following is the most likely underlying diagnosis?**

☐ A   Acute renal failure due to renal artery stenosis
☐ B   Bacterial pneumonia complicated by glomerulonephritis
☐ C   Goodpasture's syndrome
☐ D   Legionnaire's disease
☐ E   Pulmonary oedema secondary to acute renal failure

54   **A 35-year-old Afro-Caribbean man presents with a dry cough, breathlessness, malaise and arthralgia. On examination he is noted to have fine inspiratory crackles across both middle and lower lung fields, and bruising overlying both shins. His GP refers him to the Respiratory Clinic. Investigations show: creatinine 100 μmol/l, haemoglobin 13.5 g/dl, white blood cell count (WBC) 4.0 $\times$ 10^9/l, platelets 280 $\times$ 10^9/l, ESR 52 mm/h, and chest X-ray demonstrates bilateral hilar lymphadenopathy and diffuse interstitial opacification. Which of the following is the most likely underlying diagnosis?**

☐ A   AIDS
☐ B   Lymphoma
☐ C   Sarcoidosis
☐ D   Systemic lupus erythematosus (SLE)
☐ E   Tuberculosis (TB)

55   **A 24-year-old patient with a history of breathlessness on exertion and general malaise was diagnosed with pulmonary sarcoidosis six months ago. Which of the following statements regarding sarcoidosis is correct?**

☐ A   Corticosteroids are of benefit to virtually all patients at diagnosis
☐ B   Lupus pernio is a recognised skin manifestation
☐ C   Neuro-ophthalmic involvement necessitates steroid treatment
☐ D   Pulmonary sarcoidosis is commonly complicated by cardiac conduction defects
☐ E   The Kveim test is the gold standard for diagnosis of sarcoidosis

56   **A 38-year-old man with a history of asthma develops a purpuric rash, shortness of breath and haemoptysis. Investigations show: haemoglobin 11.9 g/dl, mean cell volume (MCV) 93 fl, WBC 10 × 10^9/l, neutrophils 4.6 × 10^9/l, eosinophils 1.9 × 10^9/l, monocytes 0.6 × 10^9/l, lymphocytes 2.9 × 10^9/l, platelets 200 × 10^9/l, ESR 60 mm/h, Na$^+$ 140 mmol/l, K$^+$ 4.1 mmol/l, urea 5.1 mmol/l, creatinine 100 μmol/l, and pANCA positive (perinuclear-staining anti-neutrophil cytoplasmic antibodies). Urinalysis is negative, and chest X-ray shows diffuse bilateral opacification. What is the most likely underlying diagnosis?**

☐ A   Churg–Strauss syndrome
☐ B   Extrinsic allergic alveolitis
☐ C   Goodpasture's syndrome
☐ D   Pulmonary embolus
☐ E   Wegener's granulomatosis

57   **A 52-year-old man is investigated for breathlessness. Plain chest X-ray identifies a left-sided pleural effusion, and aspiration of the pleural fluid shows the protein is 34 g/l and glucose 1.5 mmol/l. Which of the following is the most likely underlying cause of these findings?**

☐ A   Constrictive pericarditis
☐ B   Hypothyroidism
☐ C   Left ventricular failure
☐ D   Liver cirrhosis
☐ E   Rheumatoid arthritis

58   **A 14-year-old boy is referred to the Respiratory Clinic with a history of recurrent chest infections and short stature. A diagnosis of cystic fibrosis (CF) is made. Which of the following is correct in relation to this disease?**

☐   A   Diabetes insipidus is a recognised feature
☐   B   Infertility affects only male patients
☐   C   It is inherited in an autosomal recessive manner with a prevalence of 1 in 2500
☐   D   It is associated with an abnormality of chromosome 4 in most cases
☐   E   The disorder is caused by an abnormality of sodium transporter channels

59   **A 19-year-old man is referred to the Respiratory Clinic for investigation of recurrent chest infections. He has had a chronic cough productive of yellow sputum for about a year, associated with breathlessness, wheeze and fatigue. A diagnosis of bronchiectasis is made. Which of the following statements regarding bronchiectasis is correct?**

☐   A   Graves' disease is a recognised cause
☐   B   It is a recognised complication of extrinsic allergic alveolitis
☐   C   CO transfer factor is usually normal
☐   D   High resolution CT is unhelpful in most cases
☐   E   Bronchiectasis is associated with defective humoral immunity

60   **A 45-year-old university lecturer presents to the Emergency Department with fever, productive cough and haemoptysis after returning from a one-year sabbatical in Bangalore. Chest X-ray demonstrates consolidation of the right upper lung field, and sputum examination reveals numerous acid- and alcohol-fast bacilli. Which of the following statements regarding the treatment of tuberculosis is correct?**

☐   A   Cholestatic jaundice is a common complication of isoniazid therapy
☐   B   Pyrazinamide is ineffective if the patient has previously received BCG vaccination
☐   C   Response to isoniazid is determined by genetic variation
☐   D   Rifampicin can cause green discoloration of tears
☐   E   Vitamin B_{12} reduces the risk of isoniazid-induced neuropathy

61   **A 21-year-old man attends the Emergency Department with
          sudden onset of breathlessness. There is no significant past
          medical history and he is taking no regular medications.
          Chest X-ray demonstrates a large right-sided pneumothorax.
          Which of the following statements regarding spontaneous
          pneumothorax is correct?**

☐   A   Pulmonary function tests characteristically show an obstructive
         defect
☐   B   The majority of patients suffer a further recurrence within six
         months
☐   C   The optimal treatment is bedrest and analgesia
☐   D   There is a recognised association with aortic valve incompetence
☐   E   There is a recognised association with Marfan's syndrome

62   **Which of the following statements is correct in relation to
          pulmonary hypertension?**

☐   A   It is a common complication of restrictive lung disease
☐   B   It is a recognised feature of obstructive sleep apnoea
☐   C   It is associated with increased intensity of the first heart sound
☐   D   It is characteristically associated with cannon *a* waves in the JVP
☐   E   Recurrent pulmonary emboli is the most frequently identified cause

63   **You are asked to review the chest X-ray of a 20-year-old
          male medical student, taken as part of medical screening
          prior to undertaking an elective clinical attachment abroad.
          Which of the following statements is true of normal chest X-
          ray appearances?**

☐   A   The carina characteristically overlies the 6th and 7th thoracic
         vertebrae
☐   B   The heart size varies by less than 2 mm between systole and diastole
☐   C   The normal heart width is less than 40% of the thoracic diameter in
         a posterior-anterior (PA) film
☐   D   The right hemi-diaphragm can be elevated compared to the left side
☐   E   The trachea should not be deviated

64   **A 63-year-old smoker presented to his GP with a history of
          breathlessness and dry cough. A chest X-ray showed an
          abnormal opacification in the right lung field, and a
          subsequent CT scan confirmed the presence of bronchogenic
          carcinoma. Which of the following factors indicates that the
          tumour is inoperable?**

☐   A FEV_1 = 2.1 litres
☐   B   Fixed wide carina seen during bronchoscopy
☐   C   Haemoptysis
☐   D   Hypercalcaemia
☐   E   Right-sided recurrent laryngeal nerve palsy

65 **A 48-year-old woman has suffered progressive breathlessness over a six-month period. Pulmonary function tests indicate an obstructive lung defect. Which of the following disorders is most likely to account for this pattern of lung disease?**

- [ ] A Acute respiratory distress syndrome (ARDS)
- [ ] B Ankylosing spondylitis
- [ ] C Emphysema
- [ ] D Fibrosing alveolitis
- [ ] E Mitral stenosis

NEUROLOGY

Fifteen questions related to neurology topics are included in the exam. At least half of these will be on neuroanatomical knowledge, with the remainder often requiring some awareness of basic neurological science. You must spend time learning the anatomical pathways – it is not something you can work out on the day (looking at your hand will not reveal the course of the median nerve!) Topics that you must cover include:

- Anatomy (and lesions) of the cranial nerves – this appears in most papers
- Anatomy (and lesions) of peripheral nerves (in particular the hands)
- Anatomy of spinal cord (and the consequences of damage)
- Mechanisms of treatment of Parkinson's disease
- Motor neurone lesions (upper/lower/combined)
- Consequences of damage to cerebral circulation (more common recently).

66   A 32-year-old woman is admitted with a history of morning headache, vomiting and visual disturbance. She has been receiving regular treatment for acne vulgaris for the past six months, and her past history is otherwise unremarkable. You find that she has bilateral papilloedema, and cranial and peripheral neurological examination is normal. Which of the following is the most likely diagnosis?

- ☐   A   Benign intracranial hypertension
- ☐   B   Craniopharyngioma
- ☐   C   Meningioma
- ☐   D   Syringomyelia
- ☐   E   Tuberculous meningitis

67 A 42-year-old woman is referred to the Neurology Outpatient Department for investigation of unilateral proptosis. Her past history is unremarkable, and she is receiving no regular medications. On examination, temperature is 36.8 °C, pulse 92 beats per minute and BP 148/76 mmHg. Which of the following is the most likely diagnosis?

- [ ] A   Cavernous sinus thrombosis
- [ ] B   Graves' disease
- [ ] C   Lipoma
- [ ] D   Myasthenia gravis
- [ ] E   Retro-orbital lymphoma

68 A 37-year-old woman is admitted with severe headache. On examination, reflexes are brisk and symmetrical and there is mild papilloedema bilaterally. CT head scan appearances are normal. Cerebrospinal fluid (CSF) examination shows opening pressure 14 cm, and glucose 4.0 mmol/l (plasma glucose 5.5 mmol/l), protein 2.7 g/l, and microscopy shows three lymphocytes per mm^3. Which of the following diagnoses might best explain her presenting symptoms?

- [ ] A   Benign intracranial hypertension
- [ ] B   Guillain–Barré syndrome
- [ ] C   Meningioma
- [ ] D   Sagittal sinus thrombosis
- [ ] E   Viral meningitis

69 A 45-year-old woman with long-standing myasthenia gravis is admitted with a three-day history of left loin pain, rigors and malaise. She is commenced on co-amoxiclav for suspected pyelonephritis and her symptoms appear to be resolving. However, two days after admission, you are asked to review her because she is having increasing difficulty with breathing. Oxygen saturation is 88% on air and a plain chest X-ray appears normal. Other investigations show: haemoglobin 13.4 g/dl, WBC 15.6 × 10^9/l and platelets 186 × 10^9/l. Which of the following is most likely to have been the precipitating cause for her declining respiratory function?

- [ ] A   Addisonian crisis
- [ ] B   Co-amoxiclav
- [ ] C   Pneumonia
- [ ] D   Pulmonary embolus
- [ ] E   Pyelonephritis

70 A 28-year-old man presents with a history of collapse and left-sided weakness. The history does not suggest any loss of consciousness, there is no significant past medical history of note and he denies any illicit drug use. On examination he is found to have a flaccid hemiparesis affecting his left arm and leg, associated with an extensor plantar response on the left and normal reflexes on the right side. A CT head scan is normal. A diagnosis of stroke is made, and you are considering investigations for an underlying haematological cause. Which of the following statements is correct?

☐ A Anticardiolipin antibodies are a specific feature of systemic lupus erythematosus (SLE)

☐ B Factor V Leiden mutation is a recognised cause of increased stroke risk

☐ C Protein C deficiency is the commonest haematological cause of stroke

☐ D Thrombocytosis is a recognised feature of the antiphospholipid syndrome

☐ E Warfarin is contraindicated in patients < 40 years

71 A 46-year-old builder attended the Emergency Department four days ago, after falling from a ladder. At that time he was complaining of headache and nasal drip. Clinical examination was normal, and skeletal survey, including skull X-rays, were normal. After neurological observations for 24 hours he was discharged home. He is re-referred by his GP via a 999 call with persisting headache and reduced conscious level. On examination his Glasgow Coma Scale (GCS) score is 9, temperature 39.1 °C, pulse 104 beats per minute, blood pressure 92/74 mmHg, reflexes are generally diminished and there are bilateral extensor plantar responses. Which of the following is most likely to account for his current presentation?

☐ A Bacterial meningitis
☐ B Grand mal epilepsy
☐ C Subarachnoid haemorrhage
☐ D Subdural haematoma
☐ E Vertebro-basilar insufficiency

72   **A 62-year-old woman is referred to the Outpatient
            Department with a three-month history of progressive
            difficulty in walking. She has no back pain, and bowel and
            bladder function are normal. On examination, there is
            reduced power in the right leg, predominantly affecting the
            extensor muscle groups, with exaggerated reflexes and an
            extensor plantar response on that side. Pinprick sensation is
            impaired in the left leg distal to the thigh. Cranial nerve
            examination is normal. Which of the following is the most
            likely diagnosis?**

□   A   Anterior spinal artery stenosis
□   B   Brown–Séquard syndrome
□   C   Cervical disc prolapse
□   D   Syringomyelia
□   E   Vitamin B_{12} deficiency

73   **A 62-year-old man presents with transient weakness of his
            left upper limb. He is found to have weakness in a pyramidal
            distribution, associated with diminished reflexes and
            impaired sensation. CT head scan is normal. His symptoms
            and signs resolve completely within 16 hours of onset, and a
            diagnosis of transient ischaemic attack is made. He is
            discharged home on regular aspirin, and referred for carotid
            Doppler ultrasound examination as an outpatient. Which of
            the following is true?**

□   A   Bilateral endarterectomy is indicated if there are bilateral stenoses
          > 80%
□   B   Carotid bruit indicates severe underlying stenosis
□   C   Carotid stenosis > 80% indicates an annual stroke risk of over 25%
□   D   Endarterectomy is associated with 0.5–1.0% risk of stroke or death
□   E   Endarterectomy is indicated if right carotid artery stenosis is > 80%

74   **A 28-year-old man presents to the Emergency Department
            unconscious following a sudden collapse. He was previously
            fit and healthy, and taking no regular prescription
            medications. CT head scan appearances are consistent with
            subarachnoid haemorrhage. Which of the following
            statements is true of subarachnoid haemorrhage?**

□   A   CT scanning consistently identifies blood in CSF spaces
□   B   Angiography localises the site of bleeding in > 90% of cases
□   C   Hydrocephalus is recognised as a rare complication
□   D   Re-bleeding within two weeks occurs in 1–2% of cases
□   E   Vasospasm is a major cause of morbidity

75 **You are asked to review a 72-year-old man in the Emergency Department. The Casualty SHO who assessed the patient found him to have abnormal eye movements during cranial nerve examination and wants your opinion. Which of the following statements is correct?**

☐ A Impaired upward gaze is a recognised feature of Parkinson's disease
☐ B In cortical stroke, gaze is typically towards the side affected by hemiparesis
☐ C Ophthalmoplegia is a recognised feature of thyrotoxicosis
☐ D Progressive supranuclear palsy typically causes impairment of upward gaze
☐ E Voluntary gaze fixation centres are located in the temporal lobes

76 **A 27-year-old woman attends the Neurology Outpatient Clinic with a three-month history of left arm numbness and tingling. Objective clinical examination is normal. A CT head scan is normal. CSF demonstrates the presence of oligoclonal bands. Which of the following statements is correct?**

☐ A CSF oligoclonal bands are a recognised feature of SLE
☐ B CSF oligoclonal bands are of pathological significance in apparently healthy people
☐ C Electrophoresis is likely to demonstrate corresponding bands in serum
☐ D This confirms the diagnosis of multiple sclerosis
☐ E Treatment with corticosteroids should be considered

77 **A 36-year-old man is referred to the Neurology Clinic with a two-week history of weakness affecting his right arm. His past history includes left-sided optic neuritis six months ago. You consider that the underlying diagnosis is multiple sclerosis. Which of the following statements regarding multiple sclerosis is correct?**

☐ A Corticosteroids reduce the risk of further relapse
☐ B Homonymous hemianopia is a commonly recognised feature
☐ C Impaired red-green colour vision is a recognised feature
☐ D Initial presentation with motor symptoms confers a better prognosis
☐ E Onset below 40 years of age confers a worse prognosis

78   **A 65-year-old man presents to the Medical Outpatient Clinic with severe sensory neuropathy affecting both lower limbs. Thyroid and liver biochemistry are normal, VDRL test negative, vitamin B$_{12}$ 112 ng/l (normal 180–1200 ng/l). You consider the possibility that his symptoms may be attributable to subacute combined degeneration of the cord (SCDC). Which of the following is correct regarding SCDC?**

- ☐ A   Dementia is a commonly recognised feature
- ☐ B   Impaired joint-position sense is a characteristic feature
- ☐ C   It is always accompanied by raised mean corpuscular volume
- ☐ D   It is less likely in the absence of motor involvement
- ☐ E   It predominantly affects the corticospinal tracts

79   **A 71-year-old woman attends the Outpatient Clinic. Over a number of years, she has become increasingly forgetful and easily confused. On examination, there is significant cognitive impairment and her mini mental state examination score is 12/30. Neurological examination appears normal. Which of the following statements is correct?**

- ☐ A   CT scan reliably distinguishes between multi-infarct dementia and Alzheimer's disease
- ☐ B   Gait disturbance is a common early feature of Alzheimer's disease
- ☐ C   Multi-infarct dementia is more common in patients with type 2 diabetes
- ☐ D   Multi-infarct dementia is more common than Alzheimer's disease
- ☐ E   Preservation of long-term recall makes dementia less likely

80   **You see a 56-year-old woman in the Neurology Outpatient Clinic, referred for assessment of nystagmus. Which of the following statements is correct?**

- ☐ A   Downward nystagmus is characteristic of lesions at the level of the foramen magnum
- ☐ B   Patients are aware of the abnormal ocular movements in most cases
- ☐ C   Right cerebellar lesions characteristically cause nystagmus on left lateral gaze
- ☐ D   The abducting eye fails to move completely in ataxic nystagmus
- ☐ E   Upward nystagmus is a characteristic feature of benign positional vertigo

81 **You are asked to review a 52-year-old woman with multiple sclerosis who is complaining of disabling muscle spasm in her thighs and lower back. Which of the following statements is correct?**

☐ A Amitriptyline is effective in the majority of cases
☐ B Baclofen will reduce muscle tone without producing limb weakness
☐ C Diazepam should be avoided because this can promote disease relapse
☐ D Local phenol injections are associated with clinical improvement
☐ E Topical baclofen ointment is a recognised effective treatment

82 **A 48-year-old woman experiences progressive breathlessness, associated with productive cough and fever symptoms for one week. Her GP prescribes a course of amoxicillin for a presumed bacterial chest infection. However, three days later, she suffers low back pain, unsteady gait and paraesthesia of both hands and feet. On examination there is symmetrical lower limb weakness associated with generally diminished reflexes and absent plantar reflexes. Which of the following is the most likely explanation for her neurological findings?**

☐ A Brown–Séquard syndrome
☐ B Guillain–Barré syndrome
☐ C Subacute combined degeneration of the cord
☐ D Thoracic vertebral collapse
☐ E Tuberculous meningitis

83 **A 59-year-old man attends the Emergency Department complaining of left-sided facial weakness that came on earlier the same day. There is no significant past history and he is taking no regular medications. Which of the following statements is correct?**

☐ A Ipsilateral hyperacusis suggests stroke rather than Bell's palsy
☐ B More than 90% of patients make a complete recovery from Bell's palsy
☐ C Oral prednisolone may speed recovery from Bell's palsy
☐ D Stroke typically causes more extensive facial weakness than Bell's palsy
☐ E Vesicles around the left ear would suggest Bell's palsy

84   **A 17-year-old girl presents with severe frontal headache
           associated with nausea and vomiting. Her temperature is
           39.4 °C, and a blotchy erythematous rash is noted on her
           trunk and back. Clinical examination is otherwise
           unremarkable. CT head scan is normal, lumbar puncture
           opening pressure is 18 cmH$_2$O, and CSF shows a
           lymphocytosis, protein 0.14 g/l and glucose 4.6 mmol/l. Her
           serum glucose is 6.5 mmol/l and WBC 10.6 × 10^9/l. Which of
           the following is the most likely diagnosis?**

- [ ] A   Acute bacterial meningitis
- [ ] B   Acute viral meningitis due to enterovirus infection
- [ ] C   Aseptic meningitis
- [ ] D   CNS lymphoma
- [ ] E   Tuberculous meningitis

85   **You see a 54-year-old woman in the Medical Outpatient
           Clinic. She describes a four-month progressive history of
           deteriorating gait, associated with urge incontinence, urinary
           frequency and urgency. Urinalysis is negative. Which of the
           following is the most likely explanation for her symptoms?**

- [ ] A   Bladder carcinoma
- [ ] B   Frontal meningioma
- [ ] C   Multi-infarct dementia
- [ ] D   Pudendal nerve compression
- [ ] E   Thoracic spinal cord compression

86   **You see a 62-year-old man who attends the Neurology
           Outpatient Department with clinical signs of parkinsonism.
           He is not taking any regular medications, and there is no
           significant past medical history. Which of the following is
           correct in relation to anti-parkinsonian treatment?**

- [ ] A   Benzhexol is recognised as an effective treatment for bradykinesia
- [ ] B   Carbidopa monotherapy is recognised as an effective treatment
- [ ] C   Early initiation of levodopa increases the risk of 'on-off' effects
- [ ] D   Levodopa is a recognised cause of postural hypotension
- [ ] E   Entacapone acts by inhibiting dopa-decarboxylase

87 A 60-year-old woman presents to the Neurology Department for investigation of progressive limb weakness and difficulty with gait. On examination there is significant wasting of both upper and lower limb muscle bulk, and fasciculation is seen in both quadriceps. Reflexes are symmetrically brisk and both plantar responses are extensor. Sensory examination is normal. Which of the following is the most likely underlying diagnosis?

- [ ] A Alcoholic myopathy
- [ ] B Amyotrophic lateral sclerosis
- [ ] C Friedreich's ataxia
- [ ] D Progressive muscular atrophy
- [ ] E Subacute combined degeneration of the cord

88 A 53-year-old woman attends the General Medical Outpatient Clinic for investigation of progressive upper and lower limb weakness. Over the past six months she has experienced progressive difficulty with rising from her chair, climbing stairs and reaching objects above shoulder level. Which of the following metabolic abnormalities would be most likely to account for her symptoms?

- [ ] A Hypercholesterolaemia
- [ ] B Hyperglycaemia
- [ ] C Hyperkalaemia
- [ ] D Hypertriglyceridaemia
- [ ] E Hyperuricaemia

89 A 56-year-old ex-smoker presents with a one-month history of progressive weakness of proximal muscle groups and early fatiguability. His past medical history includes small-cell lung carcinoma diagnosed four months ago, and chronic obstructive lung disease. He is taking intermittent salbutamol treatment but nothing else. Which of the following is the most likely explanation for his limb symptoms?

- [ ] A Cerebral metastases
- [ ] B Guillain–Barré syndrome
- [ ] C Eaton–Lambert syndrome
- [ ] D Myopathy due to hypokalaemia
- [ ] E Spinal cord compression

ENDOCRINOLOGY

There are 15 questions on endocrinology across both examination papers. These questions may test your knowledge of normal endocrine physiology, in addition to abnormal function. You will find that most of what you need to know is contained in medium-sized textbooks of medicine. Important topics include:

- Insulin and ACTH
- Thyroxine and thyroid control
- Pituitary hormones
- Aldosterone
- FSH, LH, releasing factors
- Oestrogen and testosterone (including puberty).

90   A 53-year-old woman is referred to the Outpatient Department for investigation of galactorrhoea. She has no other symptoms, and clinical examination is unremarkable. In considering the possibility that her symptoms are drug-induced, which of the following medications is the most likely cause?

- ☐ A   Bromocriptine
- ☐ B   Co-careldopa
- ☐ C   Cyclizine
- ☐ D   Metoclopramide
- ☐ E   Tamoxifen

91   A 17-year-old Bangladeshi asylum seeker presents to her GP with malaise, weight loss and nausea and vomiting. Investigations show: Na$^+$ 127 mmol/l, K$^+$ 5.1 mmol/l, urea 14 mmol/l, creatinine 100 μmol/l, bicarbonate 15 mmol/l, and glucose 1.9 mmol/l. Which of the following is the most likely explanation for these findings?

- ☐ A   Anorexia nervosa
- ☐ B   Diabetic ketoacidosis
- ☐ C   Diabetes mellitus
- ☐ D   Insulinoma
- ☐ E   Primary adrenal insufficiency

92   **A 35-year-old woman presents to the Emergency Department
with generalised abdominal discomfort, fever and confusion.
On examination she is tachycardic and hypotensive; GCS score
is 11; temperature is 38.4 °C. Her medical notes reveal a past
history of Addison's disease. Initial investigations show: Na+
126 mmol/l, K+ 5.0 mmol/l, urea 15 mmol/l, creatinine
115 μmol/l, bicarbonate 14 mmol/l, glucose 2.0 mmol/l,
haemoglobin 11.0 g/dl, mean cell volume (MCV) 81 fl and WBC
14.6 × 10⁹/l. What is the most appropriate early management
of this patient?**

☐   A   Collect blood samples for cortisol and ACTH, followed by oral
prednisolone 20 mg daily

☐   B   Collect blood samples for cortisol and ACTH, then give
hydrocortisone 100 mg immediately, followed by intravenous fluids

☐   C   Collect blood samples for cortisol and ACTH, then perform a short
Synacthen® test

☐   D   Collect blood, urine and sputum for cultures, then intravenous
antibiotics and hydration

☐   E   Give intravenous hydrocortisone immediately

93   **A 34-year-old man has been referred to the Hypertension
Clinic with a blood pressure of 186/92 mmHg. He has been
having frequent headaches, and describes episodes of
palpitations and sweating. You are concerned that he may
have a phaeochromocytoma. Which of the following
statements is true of this disorder?**

☐   A   24-hour urinary 5-hydroxyindoleacetic acid (5-HIAA) may be useful
in diagnosis

☐   B   Beta-blockade is an appropriate first-line treatment

☐   C   Hypotension excludes the diagnosis

☐   D   It is associated with MEN 1

☐   E   It is associated with von Hippel–Lindau syndrome

94   **A 45-year-old man with established hypertension is referred to the General Medical Clinic because of sweating, frequent headaches and joint pains. The following results were obtained from an outpatient oral glucose tolerance test:**

Time (minutes)	Plasma glucose (mmol/l)	Growth hormone (mU/l)
0	8.0	5
30	12.2	8
60	14.0	14
90	12.8	26
120	11.5	18

Which of the following statements regarding the underlying diagnosis is correct?

☐ A   Colonic polyps and carcinoma are recognised associations
☐ B   He has impaired glucose tolerance rather than diabetes
☐ C   Hypocalcaemia is a recognised feature
☐ D   Insulin-like growth factor-1 (IGF-1) levels are usually reduced
☐ E   Metoclopramide is a recognised treatment

95   **One of your patients tells you that her recently born son has been diagnosed with congenital adrenal hyperplasia (CAH) secondary to 21-hydroxylase deficiency. Which of the following statements regarding this disorder is true?**

☐ A   It is associated with hypertension
☐ B   It is associated with hypokalaemia
☐ C   It may cause ambiguous genitalia in males
☐ D   21-hydroxylase deficiency accounts for around 5% of cases of congenital adrenal hyperplasia
☐ E   Virilisation of female fetuses is a recognised feature

96   **You review a 32-year-old man in the General Medical Clinic who is complaining of intermittent low back pain. His body mass index (BMI) is 35 kg/m^2. Which of the following endocrine causes is most likely to be associated with obesity?**

☐ A   Klinefelter's syndrome
☐ B   Laurence–Moon–Biedl syndrome
☐ C   Marfan's syndrome
☐ D   Noonan's syndrome
☐ E   Turner's syndrome

97 **A 28-year-old man presents with a painful anterior neck and generalised malaise. On examination, he is pyrexial (temperature 38.0 °C). There is marked tenderness and nodularity of his thyroid gland. He undergoes thyroid biopsy, and a diagnosis of de Quervain's (subacute) thyroiditis is established. Which of the following statements regarding diagnosis and treatment of this condition is correct?**

- ☐ A Antithyroid drugs are a mainstay of treatment
- ☐ B It is characteristically associated with hyperthyroidism
- ☐ C It is not associated with abnormal thyroid function
- ☐ D There is increased uptake on radionuclide scanning
- ☐ E There is usually an antecedent bacterial infection

98 **A 27-year-old woman with type 1 diabetes attends the antenatal clinic. Which of the following statements regarding diabetes in pregnancy is true?**

- ☐ A Gestational diabetes confers a 10% risk of subsequent type 2 diabetes
- ☐ B In well-controlled diabetics the risk of congenital malformation is not increased
- ☐ C Maternal diabetes is associated with neonatal hypoglycaemia
- ☐ D Pre-eclampsia is as common in diabetics as in the general population
- ☐ E Sulphonylureas do not cross the placenta

99 **You review a 16-year-old boy in the General Medical Outpatient Department. You note that he is of short stature, and investigations show: corrected calcium 1.8 mmol/l, phosphate 2.5 mmol/l, vitamin D_3 100 nmol/l, 25-OH-cholecalciferol 85 nmol/l, parathyroid hormone (PTH) 5.3 pmol/l. Which of the following statements is correct?**

- ☐ A The cAMP excretion response to PTH infusion would necessarily be reduced
- ☐ B Pseudopseudohypoparathyroidism is the most likely diagnosis
- ☐ C Rehydration and intravenous pamidronate is the treatment of choice
- ☐ D The findings are due to end-organ resistance to PTH
- ☐ E The Lundh test would be expected to confirm the diagnosis

100 **You would like to commence a 53-year-old patient with type 2 diabetes on insulin treatment. Which of the following is not a recognised treatment effect of insulin?**

- ☐ A Fatty acid oxidation in muscle
- ☐ B Glucose conversion to triglycerides
- ☐ C Glycogen synthesis in liver and muscle
- ☐ D Potassium entry into cells
- ☐ E Protein synthesis in muscle

101   **A 45-year-old woman presents with a six-month history of weight loss and heat intolerance. She is noted to have a significant goitre. Thyroid biochemistry shows TSH < 0.2 mU/l and free T4 = 27 pmol/l. Thyroid antibody titres suggest a diagnosis of Graves' disease. Which of the following statements regarding Graves' disease is correct?**

- ☐ A   Graves' ophthalmopathy is always associated with thyrotoxicosis
- ☐ B   Graves' ophthalmopathy may cause optic neuropathy
- ☐ C   In childhood it commonly causes short stature
- ☐ D   Lid lag and lid retraction are specific to Graves' disease
- ☐ E   Pretibial myxoedema is secondary to elevated circulating thyroxine levels

102   **You review a 17-year-old girl with anorexia nervosa in the Endocrinology Outpatient Clinic. Which of the following statements regarding her diagnosis is true?**

- ☐ A   Gonadotrophin-releasing hormone (GnRH), luteinising hormone (LH) and follicle-stimulating hormone (FSH) levels are elevated
- ☐ B   In female patients oestrogen levels are typically reduced
- ☐ C   It is characteristically associated with low cortisol levels
- ☐ D   Resting growth hormone (GH) levels are reduced
- ☐ E   Thyroid hormones are usually elevated

103   **A 54-year-old lady is admitted to hospital with suspected acute pancreatitis. In the past, she has had a duodenal ulcer and an episode of utereric colic secondary to a renal tract calculus. The following results are noted on the day after hospital admission: serum corrected calcium 3.0 mmol/l, phosphate 0.6 mmol/l, plasma parathyroid hormone 6.6 pmol/l. Which of the following statements is correct?**

- ☐ A   Papilloedema is a recognised complication
- ☐ B   Secondary hyperparathyroidism is the most likely explanation
- ☐ C   The biochemical findings are consistent with prolonged QT interval
- ☐ D   The patient may have multiple endocrine neoplasia (MEN) type 1 syndrome
- ☐ E   Trousseau's sign may be elicited

METABOLIC MEDICINE

Topics related to metabolic medicine are examined in the endocrinology and basic sciences questions, and typically comprise around five questions in total. Common topics include questions related to electrolyte or acid–base disturbance, diabetes mellitus and hypoglycaemia. Other important topics include:

- Control of calcium – vitamin D, parathormone, calcitonin
- Gluconeogenesis
- Mechanisms leading to hypoglycaemia
- ADH (SIADH)
- Electrolyte disturbance – hyper/hyponatraemia, hyper/hypokalaemia, hyper/hypocalcaemia
- Acid–base disturbance (also covered in respiratory medicine)
- Urate metabolism and excretion.

104   You review a 56-year-old patient with type 2 diabetes in the Outpatient Clinic. He has poorly controlled diabetes with an HbA_{1c} of 8.7%, hypertension and diabetic nephropathy. Fundoscopy in the clinic reveals proliferative retinopathy. Which of the following statements regarding his diagnosis and management is correct?

☐ A   Angiotensin-receptor antagonists are contraindicated in type 2 diabetic nephropathy
☐ B   Diabetic nephropathy is characterised by diffuse proliferative glomerulonephritis
☐ C   Immediate referral to an ophthalmologist is indicated
☐ D   Strict glycaemic control has not been found to slow progression of diabetic retinopathy
☐ E   Target BP should be < 140/90 mmHg

105   A 66-year-old lady is admitted to the Emergency Department with a GCS score of 4. She has a temperature of 35.5 ºC and pulse rate of 44 beats per minute, which is regular, and her respiratory rate is eight breaths per minute. Investigations show: TSH 14.0 mU/l, free T4 2 pmol/l, free T3 3 pmol/l. Which of the following statements regarding her condition is correct?

☐ A   Corticosteroids should not be given
☐ B   Hypernatraemia is a commonly associated finding
☐ C   Investigations are likely to show a respiratory alkalosis
☐ D   Intravenous thyroid hormone replacement is appropriate
☐ E   Iodine treatment is indicated

106 A 56-year-old man was admitted to the Emergency Department with confusion and vomiting, which had progressively worsened over the past week. Investigations show: Na$^+$ 155 mmol/l, K$^+$ 4.0 mmol/l, urea 15.0 mmol/l, creatinine 130 μmol/l, glucose 32 mmol/l and bicarbonate 21 mmol/l. Dipstick urinalysis shows glucose +++, blood +, no ketones. Which of the following diagnoses offers the best explanation for his presentation?

☐ A   Corticosteroid treatment
☐ B   Diabetic ketoacidosis
☐ C   Hyperosmolar non-ketotic state
☐ D   Renal failure
☐ E   Urinary tract infection

107 A 40-year-old lady is admitted to the Emergency Department with severe agitation. She is found to have marked tremor at rest, a heart rate of 128 beats per minute, BP 156/68 mmHg, and a respiratory rate of 14 breaths per minute. She denies any recreational drug use, and you diagnose probable thyroid crisis. Which of the following statements is true of this condition?

☐ A   Carbimazole should be avoided
☐ B   Corticosteroids are unhelpful
☐ C   Doxazosin treatment is effective for symptomatic relief
☐ D   Lugol's iodine may be effective
☐ E   Mortality rate is around 5%

108 A 26-year-old man presents with tremor and dysarthria. Urinalysis reveals glycosuria, and biochemical investigations show: Na$^+$ 140 mmol/l, K$^+$ 3.0 mmol/l, bicarbonate 17 mmol/l, glucose 4.8 mmol/l, ALT 55 U/l, AST 54 U/l, bilirubin 20 μmol/l, ALP 100 U/l. Which single diagnosis best explains his clinical presentation?

☐ A   Diabetes mellitus
☐ B   Distal (type 1) renal tubular acidosis
☐ C   Haemochromatosis
☐ D   Type 4 renal tubular acidosis
☐ E   Wilson's disease

109 A 30-year-old lady presents with left loin pain. Her only other history is that of two previous vertebral crush fractures. Her investigations show: Na$^+$ 135 mmol/l, K$^+$ 2.8 mmol/l, urea 5.7 mmol/l, creatinine 107 μmol/l, chloride 115 mmol/l and bicarbonate 9 mmol/l. What is the most likely underlying diagnosis?

- [ ] A Diabetic ketoacidosis (DKA)
- [ ] B Renal calculus
- [ ] C Type 1 (distal) renal tubular acidosis (RTA)
- [ ] D Type 2 (proximal) RTA
- [ ] E Urinary tract infection

110 A 46-year-old woman is currently an inpatient on the High Dependency Unit (HDU). You are asked to review her latest biochemistry results, which show: Na$^+$ 137 mmol/l, K$^+$ 3.4 mmol/l, urea 7.0 mmol/l, creatinine 106 μmol/l, chloride 107 mmol/l, bicarbonate 18 mmol/l. Which of the following is the most likely underlying diagnosis to account for these abnormalities?

- [ ] A Alcoholic ketoacidosis
- [ ] B Diabetic ketoacidosis
- [ ] C Prolonged diarrhoea
- [ ] D Lactic acidosis
- [ ] E Salicylate poisoning

111 A 36-year-old man is referred to the Outpatient Clinic with a five-year history of worsening pain in both knees, associated with dark sweating and staining of his clothing. He has no history of rash, alopecia, mouth or genital ulcers, or diarrhoea. He had dysuria at the age of 20 but this cleared up after treatment with oxytetracycline. On examination, there is abnormal pigmentation affecting his ears and sclerae, and there is loss of lumbar lordosis, associated with limited lumbar spine flexion. His knee joints are swollen, with bilateral effusions. Investigations showed normal full blood count and calcium. X-rays showed intervertebral disc calcification. Dipstick urinalysis showed glucose ++, protein negative. Which of the following is the most likely underlying explanation?

- [ ] A Alkaptonuria (ochronosis)
- [ ] B Ankylosing spondylitis
- [ ] C Haemochromatosis
- [ ] D Osteoarthritis
- [ ] E Reiter's syndrome

112   **Your House Officer asks you to check the results of an arterial blood gas sample collected on a newly admitted patient, which show: pH 7.49, Pao_2 12.3 kPa, $Paco_2$ 5.5 kPa, bicarbonate 34 mmol/l. Which of the following conditions offers the most reasonable explanation for these biochemical abnormalities?**

- ☐ A   Addison's disease
- ☐ B   Anxiety attack
- ☐ C   Conn's syndrome
- ☐ D   Renal failure
- ☐ E   Salicylate poisoning

113   **You see a 49-year-old man in the Metabolic Medicine Clinic. Four months earlier, he had been diagnosed with type 4 renal tubular acidosis. Which of the following is a commonly recognised feature of this condition?**

- ☐ A   Failure to acidify the urine
- ☐ B   Good response to NSAID treatment
- ☐ C   Failure of tubular ammonium (NH_4^+) excretion
- ☐ D   Hyperaldosteronism
- ☐ E   Hypokalaemia

114   **A 22-year-old woman is admitted to the Emergency Department. Immediate investigations show: Na^+ 138 mmol/l, K^+ 4.0 mmol/l, urea 5.0 mmol/l, creatinine 100 µmol/l, bicarbonate 18 mmol/l, chloride 105 mmol/l, glucose 5.0 mmol/l, plasma osmolality 307 mosmol/kg. What is the most likely explanation for these metabolic abnormalities?**

- ☐ A   Addison's disease
- ☐ B   Aspirin overdose
- ☐ C   Conn's syndrome
- ☐ D   Ethanol toxicity
- ☐ E   Type 2 renal tubular acidosis

115   **A 42-year-old publican is on holiday in southern Spain. Shortly after arrival he develops a blistering rash on his face. He had a similar rash last summer. His investigations show: haemoglobin 12.0 g/dl, WBC 8.0 × 10^9/l, platelets 82 × 10^9/l, albumin 30 g/l, bilirubin 15 mmol/l, AST 30 U/l, ALP 100 U/l and gamma-glutamyl transpeptidase (GGT) 85 U/l. Which of the following is the most likely diagnosis?**

- ☐ A   Chronic alcoholic liver disease
- ☐ B   Fixed drug eruption
- ☐ C   Porphyria cutanea tarda
- ☐ D   Sunburn
- ☐ E   Systemic lupus erythematosus

116   You review the biochemistry results of a 49-year-old woman who had recently attended the Metabolic Outpatient Clinic. These show: Na$^+$ 137 mmol/l, K$^+$ 5.0 mmol/l, urea 5.2 mmol/l, creatinine 95 μmol/l and glucose 1.9 mmol/l. Which is the best explanation for these metabolic abnormalities?

☐   A   Haemochromatosis
☐   B   Metformin treatment
☐   C   Pituitary insufficiency
☐   D   Polycystic ovarian syndrome
☐   E   Prednisolone treatment

117   A 28-year-old woman is admitted to the Emergency Department after a generalised epileptiform seizure. She has had crampy abdominal pain and vomiting for the last two days. There is a past history of depression requiring hospitalisation one year ago, but no previous seizures. She had attended her GP ten days earlier and had been prescribed a new oral contraceptive. Investigations show: haemoglobin 12.1 g/dl, WBC 12.5 × 10^9/l, platelets 370 × 10^9/l, Na$^+$ 129 mmol/l, K$^+$ 4.1 mmol/l, urea 6.6 mmol/l, creatinine 100 μmol/l. Which of the following is the most likely underlying diagnosis?

☐   A   Acute intermittent porphyria
☐   B   Drug-induced convulsions
☐   C   Encephalitis
☐   D   Hyponatraemia
☐   E   Urinary tract infection

NEPHROLOGY

A total of 15 questions related to nephrology are included in the exam. Historically, the range of topics examined has been broad. Important subjects include Wegner's granulomatosis, IgA nephropathy, Goodpasture's syndrome and renal transplantation. Your revision should also cover:

- Glomerular filtration rate (factors affecting)
- Urine discoloration (immediate and on standing)
- Water excretion and concentration
- Complement consumption
- Changes in pregnancy
- Glomerulonephritis.

118   A 29-year-old woman attends her GP with a six-month history of malaise associated with stiffness of both wrists and fingers. She is found to have a temperature of 37.3 °C, heart rate 82 beats per minute, BP 170/76 mmHg, and a facial rash. Investigations show: haemoglobin 105 g/l, WBC 8.8 × 10^9/l, C-reactive protein (CRP) 3 mg/l, ESR 72 mm/h, ANA-positive at 1/640, urea 12 mmol/l and creatinine 168 μmol/l. After contacting the Nephrology Department of the local hospital, the patient is referred for renal biopsy. What is the most likely histological features that might be identified?

- [ ] A   Focal and segmental glomerulonephritis
- [ ] B   Hypertensive nephropathy
- [ ] C   Kimmelstiel–Wilson lesions
- [ ] D   Renal cholesterol emboli
- [ ] E   Tubulo-interstitial nephritis

119   A 42-year-old man was diagnosed with adult polycystic kidney disease four years ago, and is under regular review at the Nephrology Outpatient Clinic. Which of the following are recognised complications?

- [ ] A   Acute pancreatitis
- [ ] B   Aortic valve disease
- [ ] C   Postural hypotension
- [ ] D   Subdural haematoma
- [ ] E   Ureteric calculi

120 A 48-year-old man presents to the Emergency Department with a short history of swelling and tenderness of his left calf. There is no significant past history of note, and he is taking no regular medications. On examination, the circumferences of the left and right calves are 42 cm and 37 cm respectively, and the left calf is red and tender on deep palpation. There is marked bilateral peripheral oedema and dipstick urinalysis demonstrates protein ++++ and no haematuria. Investigations show: haemoglobin 9.8 g/dl, WBC 9.4×10^9/l, albumin 16 g/l, urea 13 mmol/l, creatinine 186 μmol/l and 24-hour protein excretion of 6 g. What is the most likely explanation for impaired renal function?

- ☐ A Nephritic syndrome
- ☐ B Nephrotic syndrome
- ☐ C Non-steroidal-related nephropathy
- ☐ D Renal vein thrombosis
- ☐ E Tubulo-interstitial nephritis

121 A 20-year-old man is referred by his GP for investigation of respiratory symptoms. Ten days previously he experienced nasal congestion, and was given symptomatic treatment for suspected sinusitis. However, he has developed progressive dyspnoea associated with haemoptysis. On examination he is found to have a pulse of 82 beats per minute, BP 152/80 mmHg, respiratory rate 14 breaths per minute, and fine end-inspiratory crackles at both lung bases and mid-zones. Urinalysis shows blood ++ and protein ++, and other investigations show: Na^+ 138 mmol/l, K^+ 4.6 mmol/l, urea 12.3 mmol/l, creatinine 146 μmol/l, ANA-positive at 1/64 and cANCA-positive. Which of the following is the most likely underlying diagnosis?

- ☐ A Goodpasture's syndrome
- ☐ B Hypertensive nephropathy
- ☐ C Mesangial IgA disease
- ☐ D Rhabdomyolysis
- ☐ E Wegener's granulomatosis

122 A 60-year-old man is referred to the Emergency Department with severe lower back pain and flank bruising. He has recently been commenced on warfarin treatment for chronic atrial fibrillation but there is no other significant past medical history. On examination his pulse is 102 beats per minute, blood pressure 112/80 mmHg, temperature 37.3 °C; abdominal examination confirms flank bruising but is otherwise normal, and peripheral pulses are intact. Investigations show: haemoglobin 9.8 g/dl, WBC 9.0 × 10⁹/l, platelets 150 × 10⁹/l, INR 6.4, urea 15.2 mmol/l, creatinine 192 μmol/l, amylase 187 U/l and bicarbonate 16 mmol/l. Which of the following is the most likely cause of impaired renal function in this patient?

- [ ] A Glomerulonephritis
- [ ] B Hypovolaemia
- [ ] C Renal thromboembolism
- [ ] D Shock secondary to acute pancreatitis
- [ ] E Ureteric obstruction

123 You are asked to review a 70-year-old postoperative patient on the surgical ward. He underwent right hemicolectomy two days ago and has become oliguric. Which of the following features would most strongly favour a diagnosis of acute tubular necrosis, rather than prerenal uraemia?

- [ ] A Blood pressure 92/68 mmHg
- [ ] B Raised jugular venous pressure
- [ ] C Red cell casts seen on urine microscopy
- [ ] D Urinary osmolality of 205 mosmol/kg
- [ ] E Urinary sodium of 8 mmol/l

124 You refer a 56-year-old woman for a contrast uretero-cystogram for investigation of suspected ureteric calculus. Which of the following features is most likely to increase the risk of contrast nephropathy?

- [ ] A Asthma
- [ ] B Hypernatraemia
- [ ] C Hyperuricaemia
- [ ] D Prior overhydration with intravenous fluids
- [ ] E Theophylline

125   **You are asked to review a 24-year-old patient in the High
           Dependency Unit admitted several hours earlier, after having
           apparently taken a deliberate overdose. For which of the
           following drugs, taken in overdose, is haemodialysis most
           likely to be of benefit?**

☐   A   Amiodarone
☐   B   Digoxin
☐   C   Paracetamol
☐   D   Salicylate
☐   E   Temazepam

126   **A 52-year-old man presents to the Emergency Department
           with acute confusional state. Routine investigations show:
           urea 32 mmol/l and creatinine 412 μmol/l. Which of the
           following factors most strongly suggests chronic renal
           impairment, rather than acute renal failure?**

☐   A   Bilateral small kidneys on ultrasound scan
☐   B   Blood pressure 164/98 mmHg
☐   C   Haemoglobin 9.5 g/dl
☐   D   Potassium 5.4 mmol/l
☐   E   Proteinuria ++ on dipstick urinalysis

127   **A 19-year-old woman is undergoing outpatient investigation
           of recurrent urinary tract infections. A retrograde urethro-
           cystogram demonstrates evidence of vesico-ureteric reflux.
           Which of the following statements is correct with regard to
           reflux nephropathy?**

☐   A   Around a third of patients become dialysis-dependent
☐   B   Most cases are found in patients with abnormal renal tract anatomy
☐   C   Renal scarring virtually never occurs beyond eight years of age
☐   D   Ureteric re-implantation is often required
☐   E   Urine microscopy and culture identify bacterial pathogens in > 95%
        of cases

128   **A 75-year-old woman is referred to the Medical Outpatient Clinic for investigation of anaemia. She describes a five-month history of lethargy and tiredness, but denies any symptoms suggestive of bleeding. On examination, she weighs 45 kg and appears pale, but there are no abnormal cardiorespiratory or abdominal findings. Investigations show: haemoglobin 8.9 g/dl, mean cell volume (MCV) 88 fl, WBC 8.4 × 10^9/l, platelets 342 × 10^9/l, Na$^+$ 135 mmol/l, K$^+$ 4.7 mmol/l, glucose 8.1 mmol/l and creatinine 128 μmol/l. Liver biochemistry investigations are normal. Which of the following is the most likely underlying cause of her anaemia?**

    ☐ A   Antiphospholipid antibody syndrome
    ☐ B   Chronic renal impairment
    ☐ C   Coeliac disease
    ☐ D   Hypothyroidism
    ☐ E   Vitamin B$_{12}$ deficiency

129   **A 34-year-old woman is expecting her first child and attends the antenatal clinic for screening. There is no significant past medical history and no family history of note. Blood pressure is 138/80 mmHg, and dipstick urinalysis reveals protein ++. Further investigations show: urea 5.1 mmol/l, creatinine 90 μmol/l, and a 24-hour urine collection contains 0.4 g protein. An abdominal ultrasound scan reveals bilaterally enlarged kidneys with multiple cysts, and multiple cysts (some fluid-filled) within the liver, and is otherwise unremarkable. Which of the following statements is correct?**

    ☐ A   ACE inhibitor treatment should be introduced as soon as possible
    ☐ B   She is likely to have mutation of the *PKD1* gene, encoding polycystin 1
    ☐ C   She will become dialysis-dependent before 50 years of age
    ☐ D   Termination of pregnancy should be offered routinely
    ☐ E   Ultrasound will allow neonatal diagnosis to be established

130 A 26-year-old man complains of progressive ankle swelling for ten days, and facial swelling for one day. He has no other symptoms and no significant past history of note. There have been no infectious contacts, and he is taking no medications. Examination confirms pitting ankle and periorbital oedema, and his blood pressure is 118/60 mmHg. Urinalysis shows protein ++++, blood ++, glucose negative, and investigations find: Na^+ 130 mmol/l, creatinine 124 μmol/l, albumin 24 g/l and Ca^{2+} 1.96 mmol/l. Which of the following is the most likely underlying diagnosis?

- [ ] A Nephritic syndrome
- [ ] B Nephrotic syndrome associated with minimal-change nephropathy
- [ ] C Pyelonephritis
- [ ] D Syndrome of inappropriate ADH secretion
- [ ] E Systemic amyloidosis with renal involvement

131 A 58-year-old man presents to the Emergency Department with a one-week history of shortness of breath, haemoptysis, anorexia and generalised arthralgia. On examination, he is found to have a purpuric rash overlying both legs and there is mild peripheral oedema. Chest X-ray reveals diffuse opacification of both lower lung fields, and other investigations show: Na^+ 135 mmol/l, K^+ 5.0 mmol/l, haemoglobin 10.2 g/dl (MCV 87 fl), WBC 14.2 × 10^9/l, platelets 448 × 10^9/l, creatinine 540 μmol/l, and normal liver biochemistry. Which of the following is the most likely underlying diagnosis?

- [ ] A ANCA-associated vasculitis
- [ ] B Hepatitis C
- [ ] C Mixed essential cryoglobulinaemia
- [ ] D Sepsis
- [ ] E Toxic shock syndrome

132 A 32-year-old man is investigated for malaise and generalised weakness. Routine investigations show K^+ 2.4 mmol/l and bicarbonate 8 mmol/l. Which of the following features would most strongly suggest proximal renal tubular acidosis (type 2 renal tubular acidosis)?

- [ ] A Hyperuricaemia
- [ ] B Osteomalacia
- [ ] C Pre-existing diabetes
- [ ] D Ureteric calculi
- [ ] E Urinary pH 6.0

133 **A 46-year-old woman has recently undergone renal transplantation from a living donor. There were no technical operative complications, and she made a good immediate postoperative recovery. Two weeks later, she has developed acute renal failure. Which of the following factors is not a recognised cause of renal impairment post-transplantation?**

☐ A Captopril
☐ B Ciclosporin
☐ C Prednisolone
☐ D Ureteric obstruction
☐ E Urinary tract infection

GASTROENTEROLOGY

There are 15 questions about gastroenterology randomised across the two papers, including hepatology, biliary and pancreatic disease. One, possibly two of these will test your understanding of clinical science. Key topics include:

- Control of acid secretion (and manipulation by drugs)
- Pancreatic function and dysfunction
- Absorption and malabsorption
- Bilirubin metabolism (jaundice)
- Mechanisms leading to diarrhoea
- Gastrointestinal hormones
- Oesophageal investigations.

134   **In primary biliary cirrhosis, which of the following investigations would best confirm the diagnosis?**

- ☐ A   Abdominal ultrasound scan
- ☐ B   Antimitochondrial antibodies and liver biopsy
- ☐ C   Endoscopic retrograde choledochopancreatography (ERCP)
- ☐ D   Positive pANCA and liver biopsy
- ☐ E   Raised IgM

135   **A 40-year-old woman gives an eight-month history of generalised pruritus and intermittent pale stools. On examination, she is icteric and has spider naevi. Investigations show: haemoglobin 11.6 g/dl, WBC 8.0 × 10^9/l, bilirubin 40 mmol/l, ALT 90 U/l, ALP 360 U/l, GGT 100 U/l, albumin 34 g/l, cholesterol 9.0 mmol/l, IgG 13.0 g/l, IgA 3.0 g/l, IgM 10.0 g/l, viral hepatitis serology negative, ANA negative, and anti-smooth muscle antibody positive. Which is the most likely diagnosis?**

- ☐ A   Alcoholic cirrhosis
- ☐ B   Autoimmune hepatitis
- ☐ C   Gallstone disease
- ☐ D   Primary biliary cirrhosis
- ☐ E   Primary sclerosing cholangitis

136 **A 31-year-old Arabian man presents with recurrent episodes of abdominal pain, diarrhoea, fever, weight loss and arthritis. On examination he is thin, with a left pleural effusion and marked ankle oedema. His investigations show: haemoglobin 12 g/dl, MCV 101 fl, albumin 25 g/l, faecal fat 19 g/24 hours, and urinary xylose excretion after a 25-g oral load was 3.2 mmol/24 hours (normal 8–16 mmol/24 hours). Dipstick urinalysis shows protein +++. Which of the following best explains his presenting features?**

- ☐ A Chronic pancreatitis
- ☐ B Coeliac disease
- ☐ C Familial Mediterranean fever
- ☐ D Lymphoma
- ☐ E Nephrotic syndrome

137 **A 54-year-old man presents to the Emergency Department with haematemesis and melaena. An upper gastrointestinal endoscopy reveals a duodenal ulcer, and he tests positive for the presence of *Helicobacter pylori*. Which of the following statements is correct regarding *H. pylori*?**

- ☐ A Eradication therapy is indicated if found in a patient with peptic ulcer disease
- ☐ B It is found in 50% of patients with duodenal ulcer
- ☐ C *H. pylori* serology is a good way of assessing effectiveness of eradication treatment
- ☐ D It is associated with autoimmune gastritis
- ☐ E It may be detected by hydrogen breath testing

138 **You see a 55-year-old man with Zollinger–Ellison syndrome in the Gastroenterology Outpatient Clinic. Which of the following statements is correct regarding this disorder?**

- ☐ A It is associated with MEN 2
- ☐ B It is associated with necrolytic migratory erythema in over 90% of patients
- ☐ C It is most commonly a benign disease
- ☐ D Patients commonly present with diarrhoea and steatorrhoea
- ☐ E Secretin infusion has no effect on serum gastrin levels

139 **A 15-year-old boy presents with diarrhoea, weight loss and tiredness. On examination you notice he is of short stature and there is evidence of hyperpigmentation. He has a vesicular rash on the extensor aspect of his elbows and knees. Investigations show: haemoglobin 11.0 g/dl, MCV 84 fl, WBC 6 × 10⁹/l, platelets 150 × 10⁹/l. The blood film indicates a diamorphic appearance with several Howell–Jolly bodies and target cells seen. Which of the following statements is correct in relation to this condition?**

- ☐ A Autoantibody testing is unhelpful in establishing the diagnosis
- ☐ B Chronic pancreatitis is the most likely diagnosis
- ☐ C Jejunal biopsy is likely to show villous atrophy
- ☐ D Irritable bowel syndrome can account for these findings
- ☐ E There is no increased risk of malignancy

140 **You review a 60-year-old man with Whipple's disease in the Outpatient Department. Which of the following are recognised features of Whipple's disease?**

- ☐ A Can be diagnosed by blood and stool cultures
- ☐ B Commoner in females
- ☐ C Short courses of high-dose antibiotics are an effective treatment
- ☐ D May cause myoclonic epilepsy
- ☐ E Typically associated with symmetrical deforming arthropathy

141 **A 45-year-old woman presents with poorly localised, severe abdominal pain associated with nausea. Abdominal examination reveals guarding but no focal tenderness, and no palpable abdominal masses or organomegaly. Which of the following need not be considered in the differential diagnosis?**

- ☐ A Addison's disease
- ☐ B Familial Mediterranean fever
- ☐ C Henoch–Schönlein purpura
- ☐ D Myocardial infarction
- ☐ E Porphyria cutanea tarda

142 **A 50-year-old man has been referred to the Gastroenterology Clinic with a four-month history of diarrhoea, associated with flushing symptoms affecting the face and upper chest. You suspect possible carcinoid syndrome. Which of the following is a recognised feature of this disease?**

- ☐ A Beriberi is a recognised complication
- ☐ B Bone metastases typically produce lytic lesions
- ☐ C Cardiac involvement typically involves the left side only
- ☐ D Elevated urinary catecholamines are a diagnostic feature
- ☐ E Patients may present with exertional wheeze

143   **A 24-year-old man is admitted for elective knee surgery. He undergoes arthroscopy of his left knee. The next day, he is noticed to be jaundiced. His postoperative investigations show: ALP 95 U/l, ALT 20 U/l, bilirubin 55 μmol/l, and albumin 40 g/l. Which of the following statements regarding his condition is true?**

☐ A   Hyperbilirubinaemia is in the conjugated form
☐ B   Intravenous nicotinic acid will produce a fall in plasma bilirubin
☐ C   No specific treatment is required
☐ D   This is an autosomal recessive disorder
☐ E   Urinary bilirubin will be increased

144   **Which of the following conditions is a recognised association with hepatitis C infection?**

☐ A   Aplastic anaemia
☐ B   Migratory arthritis involving large joints
☐ C   Mixed essential cryoglobulinaemia
☐ D   Nephrotic syndrome
☐ E   Polyarteritis nodosa

145   **Which of the following statements is correct in relation to hepatitis B virus (HBV) infection?**

☐ A   80% of those infected develop chronic hepatitis B infection
☐ B   Blood levels of HBeAg correlate with infectivity
☐ C   IgG HBcAb indicates previous infection which is now cleared
☐ D   Only hepatocytes are infected
☐ E   Patients who are immunodeficient are more likely to develop fulminant hepatic failure

146   **You review a 46-year-old man with recently diagnosed liver cirrhosis. Clinical assessment, liver biochemistry and virology screening suggest he has chronic hepatitis C infection. Which of the following statements is true regarding hepatitis C infection?**

☐ A   Interferon-α clears the virus in 90% of patients
☐ B   Chronic liver disease occurs in 50–80% of those infected
☐ C   Fulminant hepatitis is common
☐ D   Hepatitis C is a DNA virus
☐ E   Transmission is usually faecal–oral

147 A 40-year-old lady has been referred to the Gastroenterology Clinic for investigation of right upper-quadrant pain. Her investigations show: ALT 92 U/l, ALP 104 U/l, GGT 35 U/l, bilirubin 22 μmol/l, IgG 17.0 g/l, IgA 2.9 g/l, IgM 2.5 g/l, pANCA positive, ANA positive, anti-smooth muscle antibody positive, anti LKM1 antibody negative, and viral hepatitis serology is negative. Liver biopsy shows evidence of piecemeal necrosis. Which of the following is the best explanation for these findings?

- A Alcoholic liver cirrhosis
- B Autoimmune hepatitis
- C Gallstone disease
- D Primary biliary cirrhosis
- E Primary sclerosing cholangitis

148 A 31-year-old relief worker presents with fever and right upper-quadrant pain. Ultrasound examination demonstrates the presence of two discrete hepatic cysts, and you suspect the diagnosis may be amoebic liver abscess. Which of the following is a recognised feature of amoebic liver disease?

- A Abscesses are commonly loculated or calcified
- B Absence of amoebic trophozoites or cysts in the stool virtually excludes the diagnosis
- C Metronidazole and diloxanide are effective treatments
- D The Casoni skin test is positive in over 90% of patients
- E The left lobe of the liver is more commonly involved than the right

149 A 50-year-old man is brought to the Emergency Department in a comatose state. He has recently returned from a one-month holiday in Spain, and is taking regular metformin for non-insulin-dependent diabetes mellitus. On examination, fundi appear normal, reflexes are brisk and symmetrical with bilateral extensor plantar responses. Investigations find: glucose 5.0 mmol/l, Na$^+$ 127 mmol/, K$^+$ 3.2 mmol/l, urea 1.2 mmol/l, creatinine 78 μmol/l. CT head and CSF examination are normal. Which of the following is the most likely underlying diagnosis?

- A Hepatic encephalopathy
- B Metformin toxicity
- C Pulmonary thromboembolism
- D *Salmonella* gastroenteritis
- E Viral encephalitis

150 **A 42-year-old man attends the Outpatient Department with a six-month history of lower abdominal pain, watery diarrhoea, and sensation of incomplete defaecation. Systemic enquiry is otherwise unremarkable. There is no history of recent foreign travel, and he is taking no regular medications. Abdominal examination is normal, and rigid sigmoidoscopy to 18 cm shows a normal mucosal appearance. Which of the following is the most likely underlying diagnosis?**

- ☐ A Colonic carcinoma
- ☐ B Crohn's colitis
- ☐ C Familial polyposis coli
- ☐ D Irritable bowel syndrome
- ☐ E Ulcerative colitis

HAEMATOLOGY

In the exam, there are 15 questions on clincal haematology and oncology, with most being disease-linked. For the clinical science questions, you should have reasonable knowledge of:

- Clotting – pathways, abnormalities, anticoagulants (see pharmacology)
- Iron, B_{12} and folate metabolism
- Outline of stem cell – differentiated cell pathway
- Haemolysis
- Methaemoglobinaemia
- ABO system and blood transfusion
- Use of blood products (fresh frozen plasma)
- Mechanisms for macrocytosis.

151 **A 42-year-old man is referred to the Haematology Outpatient Clinic for investigation of an abnormal blood test obtained during a health insurance medical examination. A copy of the test results is provided: haemoglobin 20 g/dl, packed cell volume (PCV) 70%, MCV 83 fl, mean cell haemoglobin concentration (MCHC) 31 g/dl, platelets 150 × 10⁹/l, WBC 9 × 10⁹/l. Urea and electrolytes are normal, Po₂ 11.8 kPA, Pco₂ 5 kPa. Which of the following is the most likely underlying diagnosis?**

- ☐ A Cyanotic heart disease
- ☐ B Polycythaemia rubra vera
- ☐ C Renal carcinoma
- ☐ D Sleep apnoea
- ☐ E Stress polycythaemia

152 **You are asked to review a 72-year-old woman who has undergone elective permanent pacemaker insertion earlier that day. Preoperative investigations were normal. She has become unrousable, and is found to have: respiratory rate 18 breaths per minute, heart rate 88 beats per minute, BP 104/68 mmHg and temperature 38.2 °C. Investigations show: haemoglobin 9.8 g/dl, WBC 10 × 10⁹/l, platelets 82 × 10⁹/l, activated partial prothromboplastin time (APPT) ratio 1.6 and INR 1.5. Which is the most likely diagnosis?**

- ☐ A Acute pulmonary embolus
- ☐ B Acute sepsis
- ☐ C Bacterial endocarditis
- ☐ D Disseminated intravascular coagulation
- ☐ E Hepatic vein occlusion

153   A 52-year-old man is referred for investigation of sudden
           onset of left leg swelling, and Doppler ultrasound scanning
           confirms the presence of a deep vein thrombosis (DVT). You
           note that he has recently been investigated for unexplained
           iron deficiency anaemia. His diet appears satisfactory, and
           upper gastrointestinal endoscopy and barium enema
           investigations have been found to be normal. Other
           investigations are: haemoglobin 8 g/dl, MCV 78 fl, WBC 3.1 ×
           10^9/l, platelets 92 × 10^9/l, urea 12.8 mmol/l, creatinine
           188 µmol/l and serum ferritin 86 µg/l. Dipstick urinalysis
           finds blood +++ and a trace of protein, and urine microscopy
           is unremarkable. Which of the following might best explain
           the iron deficiency anaemia in this patient?

☐   A   Coeliac disease
☐   B   NSAID-induced nephropathy
☐   C   Obstructive uropathy
☐   D   Paroxysmal nocturnal haemoglobinuria
☐   E   Renovascular insufficiency

154   A 36-year-old woman is referred for investigation of vague
           central abdominal pain. She is taking no regular prescription
           medications, and drinks approximately two glasses of wine
           each evening. Abdominal examination is normal, and there is a
           non-tender purpuric rash over both lower limbs. Investigations
           show: haemoglobin 12 g/dl, platelet count 194 × 10^9/l, ESR
           36 mm/hour, and normal liver biochemistry. Which of the
           following is the most likely underlying cause?

☐   A   Alcohol-related hepatitis
☐   B   Henoch–Schönlein purpura
☐   C   NSAID-induced nephropathy
☐   D   *Salmonella* gastroenteritis
☐   E   Systemic lupus erythematosus (SLE)

155 A 69-year-old lifelong non-smoker is referred to the Haematology Outpatient Department for investigation of abnormal blood tests, which show: haemoglobin 11.2 g/dl, WBC 86.4 × 10^9/l (98% lymphocytes), and platelets 180 × 10^9/l. On examination, his respiratory rate is 16 breaths per minute, there is widespread non-tender lymphadenopathy, 5 cm hepatomegaly and a palpable spleen. Pulmonary function tests show a forced vital capacity (FVC) of 80% (% of predicted value) and forced expiratory volume in one second (FEV$_1$) of 84%. What is the most likely explanation for the abnormal pulmonary function tests?

- [ ] A Congestive cardiac failure
- [ ] B Diffuse pulmonary lymphoma
- [ ] C Lung fibrosis
- [ ] D Pneumonia
- [ ] E Sarcoidosis

156 A 48-year-old man is referred to the Haematology Outpatient Department for investigation of abnormal blood tests, which show: haemoglobin 14.2 g/dl, MCV 112 fl, WBC 5.2 × 10^9/l and platelets 186 × 10^9/l. A bone marrow examination shows normal cellularity and microscopic appearance. Which of the following offers the most satisfactory explanation of these findings?

- [ ] A Coeliac disease
- [ ] B Folate deficiency
- [ ] C Hypothyroidism
- [ ] D Myelofibrosis
- [ ] E Phenytoin toxicity

157 A 25-year-old woman presents with widespread lymphadenopathy. She is taking no regular medications and there is no significant past medical history of note. Investigations show: haemoglobin 8.0 g/dl, WBC 42 × 10^9/l, lymphoblasts 64% and platelets 210 × 10^9/l. Which of the following is the most likely underlying diagnosis?

- [ ] A Acute myeloid leukaemia
- [ ] B Acute lymphocytic leukaemia
- [ ] C Glandular fever
- [ ] D Hodgkin's disease
- [ ] E Toxic shock syndrome

158   A veterinary medicine student attends the Emergency
            Department after being bitten by a snake. He is drowsy and
            poorly responsive. A number of bruises are noted over his
            upper limbs and trunk, and his right ankle and foot appear
            mottled and cold and are pulseless. Investigations show:
            haemoglobin 10.8 g/l, platelets 90 × 10⁹/l, prothrombin time
            24 seconds, APPT 38 seconds, fibrinogen 0.3 g/l. What is the
            most likely mechanism responsible for the abnormal clotting?

☐   A   Acute hepatic failure
☐   B   Direct activation of factor X
☐   C   Direct platelet activation
☐   D   Leiden factor V mutation
☐   E   Vascular endothelial injury

159   You are asked to review a 19-year-old man who recently
            attended screening to determine eligibility for participation in
            a clinical study. However, investigations showed:
            haemoglobin 12.4 g/dl, MCV 86 fl, WBC 3.9 × 10⁹/l and
            platelets 98 × 10⁹/l. Which of the following is the most likely
            underlying diagnosis?

☐   A   Disseminated intravascular coagulation
☐   B   Epstein–Barr viral infection
☐   C   Folate deficiency
☐   D   Idiopathic thrombocytopenic purpura
☐   E   Splenomegaly

160   A 54-year-old woman presents to the Emergency Department
            with a swollen, painful right calf. On examination, the leg is
            red and tender below the knee, and the calf circumference is
            2 cm greater than the circumference of the left calf. You
            suspect a diagnosis of deep venous thrombosis (DVT). Which
            of the following features most strongly suggests an
            alternative underlying diagnosis?

☐   A   Lymphadenitis in the right groin
☐   B   Pre-existing diabetes mellitus
☐   C   Pre-existing osteoarthritis
☐   D   Pitting oedema overlying the dorsum of the right foot
☐   E   Superficial venous dilatation overlying the right calf

161 **A 47-year-old woman is referred to the Haematology Department for investigation. Routine tests showed: haemoglobin 10.2 g/dl and MCV 112 fl. Which of the following factors most strongly suggests pernicious anaemia as the underlying cause?**

- ☐ A Impaired absorption of vitamin B_{12} after a test dose
- ☐ B Megaloblastic bone marrow appearance
- ☐ C Positive anti-intrinsic factor antibody
- ☐ D Pre-existing Graves' disease
- ☐ E Vitamin B_{12} level of 80 ng/l

162 **Which of the following is a recognised feature of haemolytic anaemia?**

- ☐ A Absence of urinary urobilinogen
- ☐ B Appearance of haptoglobin in the urine
- ☐ C Free haemoglobin in the urine
- ☐ D Increased serum conjugated bilirubin
- ☐ E Leucopenia

163 **Which of the following drugs is a recognised cause of anaemia due to antibody-mediated haemolysis?**

- ☐ A Amiodarone
- ☐ B Bendroflumethiazide
- ☐ C Diclofenac sodium
- ☐ D Morphine
- ☐ E Penicillin

INFECTIOUS AND TROPICAL DISEASES

The exam incorporates a total of 15 questions related to infectious diseases, including sexually-transmitted infections. These are often focussed on diagnostic features of specific infectious illnesses, and questions related to antimicrobial therapy. Other key topics include:

- Mechanism of action of antimicrobials, and development of resistance to them
- Disordered immunity and infection (could also be considered in the immunology section)
- Vaccination mechanisms
- Routes of transmission (faecal–oral, vectors)
- Interpretation and alteration of tuberculosis immunity.

164   **A 24-year-old woman is brought to the Emergency Department following a collapse. She is found to be moribund, temperature 39.2 °C, pulse rate 112 beats per minute, BP 91/60 mmHg. She is noted to have a widespread, diffuse erythematous rash. The WBC is 13.6 × 10⁹/l, ESR is 86 mm/hour and dipstick urinalysis shows haematuria. Which of the following statements is correct?**

- ☐   A   Blood culture would be expected to isolate *Streptococcus*
- ☐   B   Intravenous erythromycin is the treatment of choice
- ☐   C   Myalgia and raised creatinine phosphokinase are recognised features
- ☐   D   Palmar and plantar desquamation is a recognised early feature
- ☐   E   The condition is unique to women

165   **Seven patients from a local residential home are admitted via the Emergency Department with cough, fever, dyspnoea and myalgia, and diagnosed with acute pneumonia. The warden has informed you that there has been a problem with the ventilation system in the building. Which of the following is most likely to be true?**

- ☐   A   High alcohol consumption is a recognised risk factor
- ☐   B   Intravenous amoxicillin is the treatment of choice
- ☐   C   Neurological involvement is unlikely
- ☐   D   *Streptococcus pneumoniae* is the most likely cause
- ☐   E   Younger patients are at greatest risk of complications

166   A four-year-old child presents with fever, sore throat and dry cough, and develops tonsillitis. He subsequently develops dysphagia, a muffled voice, and a brassy cough. Regarding the most likely diagnosis, which of the following is incorrect?

- ☐   A   Erythromycin is commonly used in treatment
- ☐   B   The disease can be prevented using an inactivated toxoid vaccine
- ☐   C   The disease is principally spread by droplet transmission
- ☐   D   Typically causes development of a thick grey membrane over the trachea
- ☐   E   Toxin-mediated damage may affect the myocardium and nervous system

167   A 23-year-old man attends the Emergency Department with a 12-hour history of headache, fever symptoms, drowsiness, photophobia and vomiting. For the past three days he has been receiving amoxicillin treatment for frontal sinusitis. On examination, he is found to have a GCS score of 13, temperature 37.7 °C, mild neck stiffness, and a faint non-blanching purpuric rash. Which of the following is most accurate?

- ☐   A   Antibiotics should be withheld until CSF examination
- ☐   B   High-dose penicillin is the treatment of choice
- ☐   C   Hypo-adrenalism is a recognised complication
- ☐   D   Presentation is likely to be due to infection of the subdural space
- ☐   E   The rash is most likely an adverse reaction to amoxicillin

168   A 25-year-old man is bitten by a dog and develops headache, malaise and fever. He presents to the Emergency Department with flaccid paresis of all four limbs. Which of the following statements is correct?

- ☐   A   Early administration of vaccine is the treatment of choice
- ☐   B   Inhalation is a recognised route of transmission
- ☐   C   It is highly prevalent in Australasia and Antarctica
- ☐   D   Mortality is less than 10%
- ☐   E   The disease is caused by an arbovirus

169   A 15-year-old boy develops a sore throat, malaise and fever. Clinical examination reveals splenomegaly and lymphadenopathy. Which of the following is true regarding the likely diagnosis?

- ☐   A   A blood film might exclude the diagnosis
- ☐   B   A finding of EBV-specific IgM implies previous infection
- ☐   C   Heterophil antibodies appear in the early stages of the illness
- ☐   D   Rash is a recognised feature of treatment with erythromycin
- ☐   E   Corticosteroids should be avoided

170 **A 24-year-old patient develops symptoms of fever, rigors, headache and profuse sweating. He has recently returned from sub-Saharan Africa, where he suffered a number of mosquito bites. Which of the following are true regarding the most likely diagnosis?**

- ☐ A Chemoprophylaxis offers complete protection against the condition
- ☐ B Prophylaxis should be taken the day before travelling to a high-risk area
- ☐ C The disease is transmitted by the female *Anopheles* mosquito
- ☐ D The mosquito is particularly active before sunset
- ☐ E The parasite predominantly invades neutrophils

171 **A 24-year-old traveller returning from rural Nigeria develops the following clinical features: fever, sore throat, prostration, intractable vomiting, lower abdominal pain, followed by facial oedema. Which of the following is correct regarding the most likely diagnosis?**

- ☐ A Fatality is up to 25%
- ☐ B Hypertension is a common feature
- ☐ C The incubation period is typically five to seven weeks
- ☐ D The vector is an *Aedes* mosquito
- ☐ E Thrombocytopenia is a characteristic feature

172 **A 45-year-old sewage worker develops a severe flu-like illness which worsens over a few days. He develops fever, jaundice, headache and haemoptysis. On examination, he has injected conjunctivae. Considering the most likely diagnosis, which of the following is true?**

- ☐ A A small rise in transaminases is a common feature
- ☐ B Erythromycin is the treatment of choice
- ☐ C It is unlikely to produce renal impairment
- ☐ D It is caused by *Leptospira canicola*
- ☐ E It usually follows exposure to rat's faeces

173 **A 10-year-old boy from India develops a flu-like illness, followed by fever, tachycardia, headache, vomiting, neck stiffness and unilateral tremor, and finally he develops paralysis. You suspect acute polio infection because the patient reports having had contact with other patients with the condition. Which of the following is correct in relation to polio infection?**

- ☐ A Death can occur from respiratory paralysis
- ☐ B It is caused a Gram-positive coccus
- ☐ C Over 70% of patients who develop paralysis die
- ☐ D The incubation period is three weeks
- ☐ E Upper motor neurone signs are the predominant feature

174   **A 25-year-old man is bitten by a mosquito in South-East China during the rainy period. He develops encephalitis and subsequently has a large residual neurological deficit. Which of the following is untrue of this disease?**

☐ A   It is endemic in rural areas
☐ B   Patients living in rural India are at particularly high risk
☐ C   The condition is often asymptomatic
☐ D   The condition is caused by a mosquito-borne arbovirus
☐ E   The vaccine is a formaldehyde-inactivated whole-cell virus given subcutaneously over a four-week period

175   **A 45-year-old farmer is admitted to the regional Infectious Diseases Unit with a one-day history of headache, fever and vomiting. He is found to have a temperature of 38.4 °C, bilateral conjunctivitis, a petechial rash over his trunk and hepatosplenomegaly. CT head is normal. CSF microscopy shows $2–3 \times 10^6$ lymphocytes per mm^3, and CSF glucose and protein concentrations are normal. Urinalysis shows protein ++, and microscopy shows cellular and granular casts. Which of the following is the most likely underlying diagnosis?**

☐ A   Legionnaires' disease
☐ B   Lymphoma
☐ C   Miliary tuberculosis
☐ D   Sarcoidosis
☐ E   Weil's disease

176   **Which of the following statements regarding cryptosporidiosis infection is correct?**

☐ A   Causes a mild self-limiting infection in humans
☐ B   Commonly presents with abdominal pain and vomiting
☐ C   Contaminated water supplies have been implicated in outbreaks
☐ D   It is a bacterial infection due to *Cryptosporidium parvum*
☐ E   The incubation period is normally around one to two days

RHEUMATOLOGY

The exam contains 15 questions across both papers on rheumatological conditions, with overlap into metabolic (bone) conditions and immunology. Common basic science topics include:

- Normal joint physiology – synovium and fluid
- Immunology of rheumatoid disease
- Predisposition to seronegative arthropathies (HLA etc)
- Uric acid metabolism
- Mechanisms leading to osteoporosis
- Disturbed immune function in SLE
- Antiphospholipid antibody syndrome.

177   A 45-year-old alcoholic man develops a contracture of the ring finger of his right hand so that it cannot be extended. Which of the following is true with regard to the most likely diagnosis?

- ☐ A   As well as the ring fingers, thumbs are also commonly affected
- ☐ B   It can be associated with a plantar fibroma in the foot
- ☐ C   It is caused by the palmar fascial bands relaxing
- ☐ D   It is unrelated to drug ingestion
- ☐ E   It is most commonly found in patients who originate from sub-Saharan Africa

178   A 43-year-old obese man presents to his local Emergency Department after a drinking binge with severe pain in the metatarsophalangeal joint of his right big toe. Which of the following is true regarding the most likely diagnosis?

- ☐ A   Medication history is highly relevant
- ☐ B   Men and women are equally affected
- ☐ C   Positively birefringent crystals are likely to be present
- ☐ D   The presence of monosodium urate crystals is always associated with pain
- ☐ E   Urate deposits would usually be found in highly vascular areas

179   **A 45-year-old female patient regularly takes short courses of prednisolone for acute exacerbations of her systemic lupus erythematosus (SLE). Which of the following is not a recognised adverse effect of long-term corticosteroid exposure?**

☐   A   Depression
☐   B   Osteomalacia
☐   C   Peptic ulceration
☐   D   Proximal myopathy
☐   E   Striae on the trunk

180   **A 45-year-old man develops recurrent pain in the metatarsophalangeal joint of his right big toe. This usually follows an episode of binge drinking. He is prescribed allopurinol for prophylactic treatment. Which of the following are true regarding allopurinol?**

☐   A   Hypersensitivity and leucopenia and commonly seen side effects
☐   B   It is effective treatment for acute attacks of gout
☐   C   It inhibits transport of organic acids across the renal tubular membrane
☐   D   It is slowly cleared from the plasma with a half-life of 15–20 hours
☐   E   The dose should normally be 100–300 mg daily, depending on serum urate

181   **A 65-year-old man develops a swollen knee which is hot to touch and painful. Synovial fluid drawn from the joint reveals moderate numbers of polymorph leucocytes and red blood cells. Regarding the most likely diagnosis, which of the following is true?**

☐   A   It commonly occurs following intra-articular corticosteroid injections
☐   B   Corticosteroid treatment should be commenced urgently
☐   C   It is more common in young people than in older people
☐   D   It is most commonly caused by a *Pseudomonas* bacterium
☐   E   Recent trauma is a recognised risk factor

182 **A 48-year-old woman notices that the joints of her fingers have become swollen over the previous few months. Her hands have become stiff, especially in the mornings. On examination, she has hyperextended proximal interphalangeal joints and flexed distal interphalangeal joints of several fingers. She is pale, and is found to have palpable nodules along the ulnar margin of her left forearm. Regarding the most likely underlying diagnosis, which of the following is correct?**

- [ ] A   An asymmetrical polyarthritis is the most common clinical presentation
- [ ] B   Incidence is equal in both sexes
- [ ] C   May present with features resembling lower limb venous thrombosis
- [ ] D   The patient is likely to be HLA-DRW4-negative
- [ ] E   The ESR is usually normal

183 **A 40-year-old woman presents to her GP with swelling and stiffness of her fingers. She has also noticed colour changes in her hands, especially during the cold weather. She has also become aware of hair loss from her scalp and pale patches of skin that do not darken after sunbathing. Regarding the most likely diagnosis, which of the following is true?**

- [ ] A   Gastrointestinal involvement is uncommon
- [ ] B   It typically presents between the second and fourth decades
- [ ] C   It may progress to renal failure and malignant hypertension
- [ ] D   Microcytic anaemia is a common finding
- [ ] E   Raynaud's phenomenon usually develops late in the condition

184 **An 85-year-old lady is admitted to her local Emergency Department with a crush fracture of her vertebrae. Plasma calcium, phosphate and alkaline phosphatase levels are all normal. Which of the following is true regarding the likely diagnosis?**

- [ ] A   Concomitant thoracic nerve compression is a recognised feature
- [ ] B   Conductive deafness is a common feature
- [ ] C   Hypothyroidism is a recognised cause
- [ ] D   The patient should not be prescribed calcitonin
- [ ] E   Vertebral subchondral cysts and sclerosis are typical features

185 **A 45-year-old woman attends her GP complaining of tiredness and weight loss. She has also developed a rash over her face in a malar distribution. Which of the following is true regarding the most likely diagnosis?**

- [ ] A   A high neutrophil count is a common finding
- [ ] B   Antinuclear antibodies are specific for this diagnosis
- [ ] C   Glomerulonephritis is a common renal complication
- [ ] D   Hypercomplementaemia is a recognised feature
- [ ] E   It is a recognised complication of rifampicin treatment

186   **A 28-year-old man presents with a three-month history of generalised joint pains, predominantly affecting the lower back and sacroiliac joints, and urethritis. Which of the following is a recognised feature of non-specific urethritis?**

☐   A   Benzylpenicillin is the treatment of choice
☐   B   *Chlamydia trachomatis* is the most commonly identified cause
☐   C   Fewer than 25% of patients are HLA-B27-positive
☐   D   Iritis is a commonly recognised feature
☐   E   Septic arthritis is a commonly recognised association

187   **A 56-year-old woman with long-standing rheumatoid arthritis attends the Rheumatology Outpatient Department complaining of ulcers on both lower limbs. These have failed to respond to a one-week course of oral amoxicillin and topical corticosteroid treatment. Her arthritis is quiescent at present. On examination you find multiple confluent areas of ulceration overlying both shins. There is minimal redness and tenderness and no local lymphadenopathy. Which of the following is the most likely cause?**

☐   A   Amyloidosis
☐   B   Erythema nodosum
☐   C   Local vasculitis
☐   D   Pyoderma gangrenosum
☐   E   Ulcerated rheumatoid nodules

188   **A 64-year-old man complains of progressive knee pain over the past year, which is exacerbated by excessive walking. You suspect a diagnosis of osteoarthritis and arrange for X-rays of both knees. Which of the following X-ray features most strongly suggests that an alternative diagnosis might account for his symptoms?**

☐   A   Increased periarticular bone density
☐   B   Joint space narrowing
☐   C   Osteophytes
☐   D   Periarticular bony erosions
☐   E   Soft tissue swelling around the joint space

IMMUNOLOGY

Immunology has increased in the examination, which mirrors the growth in its importance in medical pratice. There will usually be four questions across both papers; of these, one will normally be on 'bread and butter' immunology, such as a question related to the features of IgA. Important topics include:

* Immunoglobulins – IgA, IgM, IgG, IgE
* Cell-mediated immunity
* Important cytokines (eg tumour necrosis factor α)
* Interferons α, β (relevant in hepatology, neurology)
* Disturbed immunity in HIV infection (question in most exams about AIDS)
* Hypersensitivity reactions
* Tissue receptor antibodies
* T lymphocytes
* Leukotrienes (eg asthma)
* Transplant immunology
* Immune complexes
* Role of complement (eg nephrology, rheumatology).

189   **You are asked to review a 29-year-old woman who presented to the Emergency Department following a collapse at home. She had been commenced on an oral antibiotic one day previously for an uncomplicated urinary tract infection. Several hours before admission she had complained of an unusual sensation in her tongue, and her partner had noted that the patient's breathing had become laboured and wheezy. Which of the following statements is correct?**

☐   A   Antihistamine treatment is of no value
☐   B   Hypertension is a commonly recognised complication
☐   C   Increased vascular permeability is a recognised feature
☐   D   This clinical phenomenon is most likely to be mediated by antigen-specific type 1 T-cells
☐   E   Hypersensitivity reactions are usually mediated by IgG

190   A 24-year-old man attends the Medical Outpatient
Department with a history of recurrent respiratory tract
infections. He denies cough or wheeze and is fit and active
between episodes. He is a non-smoker and has no risk
factors for TB. Investigations show: haemoglobin 12.8 g/dl,
WBC 8.2 × 10⁹/l, platelets 203 × 10⁹/l, IgG 8.0 g/l, IgM
0.5 g/l, and IgA 0.4 g/l. Which of the following is the most
likely underlying diagnosis?

- ☐ A   Chronic lymphocytic leukaemia
- ☐ B   HIV infection
- ☐ C   Pulmonary fibrosis
- ☐ D   Paraproteinaemia
- ☐ E   Selective IgA deficiency

191   A 38-year-old woman is admitted to the Emergency
Department with sudden onset of facial swelling and
difficulty breathing. She had one similar episode six months
earlier, which was thought due to 'aspirin allergy'. She has
been taking regular paracetamol for recurrent abdominal
pain, but no other medications. On examination, there is
some periorbital oedema and evidence of laryngeal oedema
causing stridor, temperature 37.2 °C, pulse 108 beats per
minute, BP 98/64 mmHg. Which of the following is the most
likely underlying diagnosis?

- ☐ A   Acute epiglottitis
- ☐ B   Acute intermittent porphyria
- ☐ C   C1 esterase inhibitor deficiency
- ☐ D   Delayed paracetamol allergy
- ☐ E   Paracetamol overdose

192   You review a 45-year-old man in the Infectious Diseases
Outpatients Department. He was diagnosed with HIV
infection three years ago, and is taking three antiretroviral
treatments in combination. Which of the following is likely to
provide the most useful prognostic information?

- ☐ A   CD4:CD8 cell ratio
- ☐ B   IgG levels
- ☐ C   Lymphocyte count
- ☐ D   Total CD4 count
- ☐ E   Viral load

193 **You are asked to give advice to a ward nurse regarding the usage of vaccines. Which of the following is correct in relation to the use of bacille Calmette–Guérin (BCG) and yellow fever vaccines?**

- [ ] A If both vaccines are required it is best to give them either simultaneously or three weeks apart
- [ ] B Mild febrile and any non-systemic illness are strict contraindications
- [ ] C They are generally regarded as being safe in pregnancy
- [ ] D They should not be given for at least three days after blood transfusion
- [ ] E They are usually stored at room temperature

194 **You are considering administering vaccine to a 25-year-old patient with immunosuppression due to HIV infection. Which one of the following vaccinations would be regarded as comparatively safe?**

- [ ] A Measles
- [ ] B Mumps
- [ ] C Oral polio
- [ ] D Tetanus
- [ ] E Yellow fever

195 **A 45-year-old man is given immunosuppressant therapy following a kidney transplant. An increase in serum urea and creatinine is found four months postoperatively. He also complains of tremor, paraesthesiae, fatigue and gingival hypertrophy. You consider that his renal impairment and symptoms may be caused by ciclosporin treatment. Which of the following is true regarding of ciclosporin therapy?**

- [ ] A Gingival hyperplasia is a recognised side effect
- [ ] B It acts predominately on B lymphocytes
- [ ] C It has good absorption following oral administration
- [ ] D Its main mode of action is bone marrow suppression
- [ ] E The daily dose is usually 50–60 mg/kg

STATISTICS

The fear that statistics generates is entirely out of proportion to its representation in the exam. Typically, only one or two questions are included as a basic sciences topic. However, the range of questions included in the exam is narrow and, with a little preparation, it is possible to gain some marks in this section. Important topics include:

- Definitions of mean, median and mode
- Standard deviations, errors
- When to apply parametric and non-parametric tests
- Correlation coefficients (r or R)
- Normal distributions (including t-distribution) and skewed distributions
- Tests of significance (probability).

You might also want to considersome more recent developments:

- Confidence intervals and limits
- Risk – relative and absolute, number needed to treat (evidence-based medicine)
- Clinical trials.

196   You attend a Grand Rounds presentation at your local hospital, where the Radiology Department presents data regarding referrals investigation. A study has found that the correlation between the age of the patient and the likelihood of haemorrhage on CT head scan has an *R* value of 0.8 and a *P* value < 0.001. Which of the following is correct?

- ☐   A   CT scan investigations should be performed more often in younger patients
- ☐   B   Older patients are more likely to have brain haemorrhage than younger ones
- ☐   C   The *p*-value indicates that insufficient cases were included
- ☐   D   There is a linear relationship between the measures
- ☐   E   There is no statistical correlation between the measures

197   **You are reviewing data presented in the *British Medical Journal* about a new test for Alzheimer's disease. The authors of the paper have presented the data as mean values ± standard deviations. Which of the following is true regarding standard deviation?**

☐   A   It is calculated as the square of the variance
☐   B   It is generally more difficult to interpret than standard error of the mean
☐   C   It is a measure of repeatability of the test
☐   D   It is a measure of dispersion of measurements from the mean value
☐   E   It reduces inaccuracy when analysing skewed data

198   **A doctor wishes to set up a screening programme to screen for gastric cancer in his hospital. Which of the following is most relevant in designing and implementing an effective screening programme?**

☐   A   Knowledge of the natural history of the disease is unimportant
☐   B   The screening test need not have been provdn safe
☐   C   The test should be widely applicable across unselected populations
☐   D   The test should identify patients who require further investigation or treatment
☐   E   The test should primarily be used to determine prognosis

199   **An occupational physician hypothesises that gaseous emission from a local factory is causing the high level of respiratory illness found in the local area. Which of the following factors would most strongly implicate the gas as a causal factor?**

☐   A   Duration of exposure appears to be related to disease risk
☐   B   Findings from previous studies at other locations found no association
☐   C   No potential biological mechanism has been identified
☐   D   The incidence of respiratory illness increased before gas emissions occurred
☐   E   The prevalence of heavy tobacco use is higher in the area

200   Observational studies have suggested that there may be a higher incidence of lymphoreticular disorders in people living in close proximity to high-voltage electricity pylons. You wish to design a prospective case-control study to explore whether there might be a causal link. Which of the following is the most important consideration in relation to using a case-control design in this setting?

☐ A It is likely to be more expensive than a cohort study
☐ B It would be prone to bias
☐ C It is particularly suited to illnesses with a short latent period
☐ D Validity would be affected by subject dropouts during follow-up
☐ E It would identify a temporal relationship between exposure and illness

201   A clinician has finished a trial of a new analgesic for long-term pain comparing it to placebo. The following results are obtained. Mean pain score after three months of treatment, where 0 = no pain and 10 = severe pain: active treatment = 3.0, placebo = 4.5 ($P = 0.3$), and 95% confidence intervals for the difference in scores = −3 to 5.2. Which of the following statements is most accurate?

☐ A Active treatment and placebo are equally effective
☐ B The 95% confidence interval is calculated as 2.58 standard errors of the mean (SEM)
☐ C The best statistical test in this situation is the chi-square test
☐ D The trial result is not statistically significant
☐ E There is a 30% chance that the analgesic is more effective than placebo

DERMATOLOGY

There are eight questions on dermatology across both papers. Mostly, these will be disease-related, but some may test your knowledge of disordered immunity. You should consider:

- Skin manifestations of systemic disease
- Immunology and the skin
- Vasculitides – mechanisms
- Blistering skin conditions
- Koebner's phenomenon.

202 **A 44-year-old epileptic man attends his GP with an exacerbation of psoriasis. He has also taken various types of medication over the years for depression and agitation and has recently had an increasing number of epileptic seizures. Which of the following drugs is likely to have contributed to his seizures and psoriatic exacerbation?**

- ☐ A Clozapine
- ☐ B Diazepam
- ☐ C Dothiepin
- ☐ D Fluoxetine
- ☐ E Lithium

203 **A 35-year-old patient with AIDS develops white, spongy, slightly raised lesions inside his mouth. He also develops flat-topped papules on the inner wrist area, which are bluish-red and are very itchy, and you suspect a diagnosis of lichen planus. Which of the following is correct with regard to lichen planus?**

- ☐ A High-potency topical steroids will have no effect on the plaques
- ☐ B It is entirely benign
- ☐ C It should always be treated, even if asymptomatic
- ☐ D The Koebner phenomenon is a recognised feature of active disease
- ☐ E The nails are always unaffected

204   **An 18-year-old farmworker develops a rapidly growing, solitary red papule on his hand. He started working with sheep a few weeks previously. Which of the following is true regarding the underlying diagnosis?**

☐   A   A similar clinical picture may occur in patients who have contact with cows

☐   B   Clinically the patient may be pyrexial and have local lymphadenopathy

☐   C   Lesions will always persist indefinitely without appropriate treatment

☐   D   The condition is usually caused by infection with a streptococcal bacterium

☐   E   The incubation period is four to five weeks

205   **A three-year-old boy is seen at a Dermatological Outpatient Department with elevated, smooth reddish papules, each having a small central punctum, on his face. Which of the following is true regarding the most likely diagnosis?**

☐   A   Curettage of the lesions should be avoided

☐   B   It is as common in the elderly as in young patients

☐   C   It is caused by a pox virus

☐   D   It is common in agricultural workers due to contact with sheep

☐   E   It is frequently associated with malignancy

206   **A 15-year-old boy attends his GP with dry, uncomfortable feet that have become fissured. Which of the following is true regarding the most likely diagnosis?**

☐   A   The condition is a type of allergic dermatitis

☐   B   The condition may occur in very small babies

☐   C   The discomfort is typically worst in fissured areas

☐   D   The lateral aspect of the foot is typically affected

☐   E   Wearing synthetic footwear will help the condition

MOLECULAR AND GENETIC MEDICINE

Around five questions will be dedicated to molecular biology and genetics in the exam, as a basic science topic. Many candidates find these difficult but, as the College has pointed out, the knowledge tested is regularly covered by reviews and editorials in the prime medical journals (*Lancet*, *British Medical Journal* and the *New England Journal of Medicine*). If you have time, you may want to look through some back copies of these. You should remember, however, that the exam is set a year in advance and topical items will not appear. Some things that you might want to consider include:

- Definition of terms (eg introns, exons etc)
- Polymerase chain reactions
- Genetic predisposition to disease
- Linkages
- Oncogenes
- Mitochondrial DNA function
- Genetic anticipation.

207   In addition to contributing to the structural integrity of blood vessels, the endothelium is responsible for a number of physiological mechanisms involved in the regulation of the cardiovascular system. Which of the following statements regarding the vascular endothelium is correct?

- ☐ A   Acetylcholine inhibits endothelial nitric oxide liberation
- ☐ B   Endothelium-derived nitric oxide stimulates smooth muscle contraction
- ☐ C   Endothelial dysfunction causes reduced platelet aggregatability
- ☐ D   LDL cholesterol does not have a direct influence on endothelial function
- ☐ E   Reduced nitric oxide liberation is a recognised feature of diabetes mellitus

208 **Which of the following statements in relation to the Human Genome Project is correct?**

☐ A Around 40% of nucleotides in human DNA contribute to the genetic code

☐ B Leber's optic atrophy is usually associated with a single point DNA mutation

☐ C Screening is suited to disorders caused by non-recurring point mutations

☐ D The human genome contains approximately 1500 genes

☐ E There are around 500,000 nucleotides in haploid human DNA

209 **A 54-year-old man attends the Medical Outpatient Clinic for review of his current hypertension treatment. You note that he has multiple *café-au-lait* spots over his trunk and upper limbs, and multiple discrete nodules within the skin. Which of the following is correct with respect to neurofibromatosis?**

☐ A Acoustic neuroma is a characteristic feature of neurofibromatosis type 2

☐ B Neurofibromatosis type 2 is now the most commonly recognised form

☐ C The incidence of neurofibromatosis is around 0.5–1.0%

☐ D The *NF1* gene responsible for neurofibromatosis type 1 encodes schwannomin

☐ E There is virtually complete genetic penetrance in neurofibromatosis type 1

210 **Which of the following is correct with respect to the molecular genetics of haemophilia A?**

☐ A Factor VIII is reduced to 10–20% of normal, and this is associated with spontaneous bleeding

☐ B Inheritance is Mendelian in an autosomal recessive pattern

☐ C Recombinant factor VIII is not yet available

☐ D The gene for factor VIII was cloned in 1984

☐ E There is a positive family history in more than 90% of patients

ANSWERS AND TOPIC SUMMARIES

CARDIOLOGY

1   A: Amiodarone toxicity
The patient has biochemical evidence of hepatitis and hyperthyroidism. A restrictive lung defect and reduced CO transfer are consistent with interstitial lung disease, for example pulmonary fibrosis. Although heart failure can cause hepatitis and diminished CO transfer, this is less likely given the normal appearance on echocardiography. Pneumonia would not adequately explain the abnormal liver function tests (LFTs), and hyperthyroidism alone would not explain the patient's abnormal pulmonary function tests (PFTs) and hepatitis. Hereditary haemochromatosis is an autosomal recessive disorder, in which there is increased iron absorption leading to overload and tissue deposition. It could account for the skin discoloration and hepatitis, but would not fully account for the abnormal PFTs in the absence of heart failure, or the TFTs.

Amiodarone is a class III anti-arrhythmic that is used to treat supraventricular and ventricular tachyarrhythmias. There are a number of recognised adverse effects, particularly seen in long-term use: deranged thyroid biochemistry, photosensitivity (skin and ocular), hepatitis, peripheral neuropathy, pulmonary fibrosis, corneal microdeposits, metallic taste in the mouth, skin discoloration (slate-grey pigmentation), arrhythmia, ataxia, optic neuritis, myopathy and epididymitis.

2   A: The absence of P waves
It is often difficult to distinguish ventricular tachycardia (VT) from supraventricular tachycardia (SVT). With the latter, there may be 'aberrant conduction' at high heart rates, possibly due to cardiac ischaemia, giving rise to broad ventricular complexes. The distinction is important because VT responds favourably to DC cardioversion, which should be given urgently if there is haemodynamic compromise. The presence or absence of P waves is often difficult to distinguish, but is very specific. The following features favour VT rather than SVT:

*   Past history of ischaemic heart disease
*   Capture beats (intermittent sinoatrial (SA) node complexes transmitted to the ventricle)
*   Fusion beats (composite of activity arising from ventricle and SA node)
*   Atrioventricular (AV) dissociation
*   Left axis deviation (LAD)
*   QRS duration > 0.14 s
*   Concordance of QRS complexes across the chest (V) leads
*   History of ischaemic heart disease (IHD)
*   Variable S1 morphology
*   Not terminated by carotid sinus massage or adenosine.

3   E: Sotalol
A broad range of drugs and metabolic disturbances can cause QT prolongation, including hypokalaemia, hypocalcaemia, hypomagnesaemia, hypothermia, anti-psychotic drugs, erythromycin, and the class III anti-arrhythmic drugs, amiodarone and sotalol. The QT interval is inversely related to heart rate, and a number of correction formulae are used to negate the effects of heart rate. Most commonly, Bazett's correction is used: $QT_c = QT/\sqrt{(R{-}R \text{ interval})}$. Drugs such as verapamil, diltiazem and β-blockers prolong the QT interval, but have less effect on QT_c. Sotalol is the most probable cause of a substantially prolonged QT interval due to its action as a class III anti-arrhythmic and its effects on heart rate. Ischaemic heart disease can be associated with QT prolongation, but this is uncommon and less obvious than its effects on depolarisation and conduction events.

Hyperkalaemia characteristically causes:

- Tall tented T waves
- Small or absent P waves
- Increased PR interval, widened QRS complex
- Sine wave pattern
- Ventricular fibrillation
- Asystole.

4   B: Nodal or junctional rhythm
Cannon waves are produced when the atrial contraction coincides with a closed tricuspid valve, typically due to concurrent ventricular systole. This situation arises in a number of circumstances:

- Nodal or junctional rhythm
- Complete AV heart block
- Single-chamber ventricular pacing
- Ventricular tachycardia
- Ventricular extrasystoles.

Only in the case of nodal or junctional rhythms do cannon waves arise with every heartbeat, which is a more reasonable explanation of 'regular' cannon waves. The other causes are associated with intermittent cannon waves because atrial and ventricular systole coincide in a more unpredictable manner.

5   D: Isosorbide mononitrate
ISIS-4 and GISSI-3 were large prospective studies that found nitrate therapy to have no effect on subsequent cardiovascular mortality. They are thought to be effective for symptomatic relief only. Beta-blockers, angiotensin converting enzyme (ACE) inhibitors and β-hydroxy-β-methylglutaryl-CoA-reductase (HMG CoA-reductase) inhibitors have all been shown to improve survival and reduce the risks of future cardiovascular events in large prospective trials. Atorvastatin has not been studied directly in this setting, but is expected to offer the same benefits as other 'statins'.

6   E: Valsartan

There is mounting evidence that β-blockers improve survival in patients with severe heart failure (bisoprolol, carvedilol and metoprolol) but benefits in unselected patients or in those with mild to moderate heart failure are less certain. Digoxin and furosemide have beneficial haemodynamic effects that can improve symptoms and reduce hospitalisation, but do not confer improved survival in congestive heart failure (CHF). Spironolactone has been shown to confer a modest but important improvement in survival among congestive heart failure patients who were already receiving other treatments. Blockade of the renin-angiotensin-aldosterone system reduces cardiac remodelling, improves cardiac performance and substantially enhances survival in congestive heart failure. The benefits of ACE inhibitors have long been established, whereas supportive evidence for angiotensin-II receptor antagonists has only recently become available, (eg for valsartan in the ValHeFT study).

7   D: Statins lower LDL cholesterol and triglyceride concentrations

Epidemiological studies indicate that cardiovascular and coronary heart disease risk is closely related to triglyceride and total very low density lipoprotein (VLDL) and LDL cholesterol concentrations, and inversely related to HDL cholesterol concentrations. Most evidence suggests that improved outcome is associated with the extent of cholesterol reduction. Statins inhibit HMG CoA-reductase, the rate-limiting enzyme in cholesterol synthesis, which is normally most active overnight. Adverse rather than therapeutic effects of statins include myopathy and derangement of liver biochemistry, and the risk of each appears to be dose-dependent. Statins lower triglyceride concentrations, LDL and total cholesterol concentrations, and increase HDL concentrations. Dietary cholesterol restriction will increase the pharmacological effects of lipid-lowering therapy.

Statins have been shown to reduce the risk of coronary events in those with normal cholesterol (TEXCAPS and CARE studies). They reduce mortality in those with a cholesterol > 4 mmol/l and no clinical history of cardiovascular disease (WOSCOPS study) or established coronary heart disease (4S study).

8   B: Bacterial endocarditis

The clinical signs are indicative of right heart failure with pulmonary incompetence. These signs are compatible with alcohol-related cardiomyopathy but this does not adequately explain the fever and the clinical history is comparatively short. Infiltrative cardiac disease, including sarcoidosis, often presents with more prominent features of left heart failure. The most probable explanation is bacterial endocarditis affecting the right heart. In a young adult, this is often a complication of intravenous drug misuse, but carcinoid syndrome is also a possibility. In older patients, the possibility of a gastrointestinal source of sepsis must be considered.

9   E: Right bundle branch block
Dextrocardia can cause a similar appearance but is a much less common cause, and rarely presents as an isolated ECG abnormality. Other causes include Wolff–Parkinson–White syndrome type A, right ventricular hypertrophy, posterior myocardial infarction, incorrect lead placement, and Duchenne muscular dystrophy. Right bundle branch block can be a normal feature or, in other cases, a manifestation of conduction system disease and the possibility of ischaemic heart disease might require consideration.

10   C: Slurred upstroke of the QRS complex
The clinical scenario is typical of supraventricular tachycardia (SVT), which usually occurs in short-lived episode(s) and is not characteristically associated with any important underlying abnormality or adverse clinical consequences. A slurred QRS upstroke (δ wave) appearance and/or abnormally a short PR interval suggests the presence of an aberrant conduction pathway between atria and ventricles, as found in Wolff–Parkinson–White syndrome. This poses the risk of ventricular fibrillation should atrial fibrillation ensue. The narrow-complex tachycardia may be terminated by intravenous adenosine. Digoxin and verapamil can accelerate conduction down the accessory pathway by blocking the AV node and are contraindicated. Drug management includes β-blockers, flecainide and amiodarone. Radiofrequency ablation is an accepted first-line treatment.

11   C: It is a recognised sign of severe mitral incompetence
A third heart sound may be physiological or pathological, and is typically heard shortly after the second heart sound. It is thought to reflect abnormally high blood flow across the AV valves during passive ventricular filling and can occur in hyperdynamic states, including hyperthyroidism, anaemia and pregnancy. A pathological third heart sound is due to rapid ventricular filling and may be heard in mitral regurgitation, ventricular septal defect (VSD), cardiomyopathy, constrictive pericarditis and congestive heart failure. In contrast, a fourth heart sound is always pathological. It occurs during late diastole in association with atrial contraction and, therefore, is not present in atrial fibrillation. A fourth heart sound reflects a stiff, non-compliant left ventricle as found in systemic hypertension, left ventricular hypertrophy (LVH), hypertrophic cardiomyopathy and cardiac amyloid.

12   E: Widespread bifid P waves on the ECG
This finding (P mitrale) suggests the presence of left atrial hypertrophy, which is suggestive of mitral valve disease. In contrast, widespread peaked P waves (P pulmonale) is consistent with right atrial hypertrophy secondary to pulmonary hypertension and thromboembolic disease. The other features are in keeping with raised pulmonary pressure and recurrent pulmonary emboli.

13 B: Clinical signs of chronic liver disease

The amount of alcohol, type of alcohol and pattern of drinking associated with alcohol-related cardiomyopathy are highly variable. Evidence of chronic liver disease suggests end-organ damage elsewhere and is in keeping with the diagnosis. Liver biochemistry disturbances are non-specific and can be a transient finding after an acute alcohol binge, regardless of the presence of any significant end-organ damage. Arrhythmia is common in alcoholic cardio-myopathy, for example atrial fibrillation, along with hypertension and a dilated pattern of cardiomyopathy.

14 C: Narrow pulse pressure

A narrow pulse pressure (systolic – diastolic BP) suggests a severe aortic valve stenosis. This might be accompanied by a slow-rising carotid pulse character, which is less reliable and can be mistakenly identified in the presence of significant carotid atherosclerosis. Severe aortic stenosis can be associated with a murmur of very low intensity. Other indicators of severe aortic stenosis are left ventricular hypertrophy or failure, diminished intensity of the aortic component of the second heart sound, and a precordial thrill.

15 D: Double apical impulse

Hypertrophic cardiomyopathy (HCM) is an inherited cardiac muscle disorder that affects sarcomeric proteins, resulting in small vessel disease, myocyte and myofibrillar disorganisation, and fibrosis, with or without myocardial hyper-trophy. Hypertrophy and disordered myocardial contraction can result in subvalvular aortic outflow obstruction. HCM can result in significant cardiac symptoms due to haemodynamic compromise or arrhythmia, including breathlessness, angina, syncope and sudden death. Before the identification of the disease-causing genes, the World Health Organisation defined HCM as left or bi-ventricular hypertrophy in the absence of any cardiac or systemic cause. However, it is now recognised that hypertrophy is absent in up to 20% of gene carriers. Other signs include a jerky pulse, which may be low-volume in the presence of significant outflow obstruction, a fourth heart sound, a prominent *a* wave in the jugular venous pressure trace, and murmur intensity decreased on squatting but increased on standing. HCM is often accompanied by mitral incompetence.

Diagnosis is based on characteristic ECG and echo abnormalities. The detection of a significant gradient across the left ventricular outflow tract (LVOT) will guide treatment. Holter monitoring may help detect arrhythmias in certain cases, and angiography is often required to assess outflow obstruction and identify coronary artery disease.

16   D: Right axis deviation on the ECG
ASD is the commonest congenital defect detected in adulthood, and ostium
secundum defects account for around 70%. They are due to fossa ovalis defects.
Surgical closure should be considered in young adults with symptoms, a
significant shunt (pulmonary to systolic blood flow ratio > 1.5:1) and normal
pulmonary artery pressure. ASD may present with palpitations, shortness of
breath, fatigue or paradoxical embolisation. Atrial arrhythmias are common, even
after surgical correction. The risk of endocarditis is low, isolated ostium secundum
ASDs do not require antibiotic prophylaxis. Progressive pulmonary hypertension
can lead to right heart failure (Eisenmenger's syndrome). ASD is associated with
mitral valve prolapse in 10–20% of cases, and recognised features include right
bundle branch block (RBBB) and right axis deviation on the ECG, a tricuspid
diastolic murmur, wide fixed splitting of the second heart sound, a pulmonary
systolic murmur, and plethoric lung fields on plain chest X-ray (CXR).

17   D: A loud pulmonary component of the second heart sound (P2)
P2 is usually quiet or inaudible. Tetralogy of Fallot is the most common form of
cyanotic congenital heart disease. It consists of:

- Ventricular septal defect (VSD)
- Right ventricular hypertrophy
- Pulmonary stenosis
- An overriding aorta.

Patients usually present after six months old. Clinical features include:

- Cyanotic attacks with syncope
- Clubbing
- Right ventricular heave
- Pulmonary systolic thrill
- Ejection systolic murmur over pulmonary area
- Inaudible or quiet P2
- Right ventricular hypertrophy (RVH) on ECG.

CXR may show a boot-shaped heart, pulmonary oligaemia, a large aorta and
small pulmonary artery. Possible complications include:

- Arrhythmias and sudden death
- Right ventricular dysfunction
- Endocarditis
- Polycythaemia
- Coagulopathy
- Paradoxical embolism
- Cerebral abscess.

Children can undergo correction at an early age. Previously the practice was for
individuals to undergo some form of palliative procedure to allow a period of
growth before surgery, such as a   Blalock–Taussig shunt, or a Waterston or
Potts' anastomosis.

18   D: Coarctation of the aorta

Aortic coarctation accounts for about 5% of cases of congenital heart disease. It is more common in males and is usually distal to the origin of the left subclavian artery. Patients usually present in infancy, or before the third decade, with heart failure. There are recognised associations with: bicuspid aortic valve, patent ductus arteriosus, ventricular septal defect, mitral valve disease, cerebral aneurysm, Turner's syndrome and renal malformations. Recognised complications are headache, stroke, heart failure, ischaemic heart disease, aortic dissection and infective endocarditis. Surgical correction is associated with a 5–10% recurrence rate.

19   B: Myocardial thickening on echo

Myocardial thickening is seen in restrictive cardiomyopathy. Pericardial thickening is seen in constrictive pericarditis (usually on computed tomography (CT) or magnetic resonance imaging (MRI)). Constrictive pericarditis occurs as a result of chronic pericardial inflammation. This causes fibrotic thickening of the pericardium that is usually associated with fusion of the visceral and parietal pericardium, which obliterates the pericardial space. Causes include:

- TB (usually post-pericardial effusion)
- Mediastinal radiotherapy
- Malignancy
- Prior purulent pericardial effusion
- Post-pericardiotomy
- Post-viral pericarditis
- Drugs, eg hydralazine
- Connective tissue diseases, eg rheumatoid arthritis, systemic lupus erythematosus (SLE)
- Post-uraemic pericarditis
- Idiopathic.

Patients usually present with symptoms and signs of chronic heart failure. Examination reveals a high jugular venous pressure (JVP) which classically demonstrates Kussmaul's sign. Heart sounds are soft apart from a pericardial knock, the result of rapid ventricular filling during early diastole. Volume overload with pleural effusions, hepatic engorgement, ascites and marked peripheral oedema are common. Pulsus paradoxus occurs rarely and indicates the presence of a coexisting tense effusion. CXR reveals pericardial calcification in about 50% of patients. ECG reveals generalised T-wave flattening and low-voltage QRS complexes. Echo reveals reduced left ventricular diastolic wall motion and abnormal septal motion. CT and MRI assess thickening and calcification of the pericardium. Cardiac catheterisation reveals equalisation of end-diastolic pressures in all four chambers. The differentiation from restrictive cardiomyopathy and cardiac tamponade may be difficult. Constrictive pericarditis is treated by pericardial resection.

20   C: It increases stroke volume and cardiac output

Digoxin is a K^+/Na^+ ATPase inhibitor. It acts predominantly at the atrioventricular node to increase the refractory period and, therefore, is useful in the control of ventricular rate in atrial tachycardias and fibrillation. It is a positive inotrope, and is particularly useful in patients with atrial fibrillation and coexisting heart failure. Digoxin leads to haemodynamic improvements, symptom relief and less need for hospitalisation, but has not been found to have a significant impact on mortality. It is contraindicated in complete heart block, second-degree heart block, Wolff–Parkinson–White syndrome and hypertrophic cardiomyopathy. Adverse effects include arrhythmia, heart block, nausea and vomiting, diarrhoea, headache, confusion, xanthopsia and gynaecomastia. Life-threatening toxicity can be treated with digoxin-specific F_{ab} antibody fragment.

CLINICAL PHARMACOLOGY

21   D: Moxonidine
Moxonidine is a centrally acting antihypertensive agent that is usually reserved for resistant cases. Postural hypotension is a frequent complication of treatment, particularly in elderly patients. Lisinopril, in common with other ACE inhibitors, can cause first-dose hypotension and dose-dependent postural hypotension. Therefore, ACE inhibitors are introduced at low dose and titrated depending on BP response and tolerability. Beta-blockers do not cause postural hypotension but can exaggerate the effect of other drugs by reducing compensatory sympathetic responses. Alpha-receptor antagonists, for example doxazosin, often cause postural hypotension, particularly in high doses, and this is a recognised feature of vasodilating (dihydropyridine) calcium-channel blockers such as nifedipine. In practice, the temporal relationship between adverse effects and initiation of treatment can help to identify the causal drug.

22   C: Erythromycin
Warfarin is cleared by hepatic metabolism. Erythromycin is a powerful hepatic enzyme inhibitor, which delays metabolism of warfarin and thereby potentiates its effects. Omeprazole is a potential cause, but causes less powerful inhibition of hepatic enzymes. Other important hepatic enzyme inhibitors known to potentiate the effects of warfarin include cimetidine, ciprofloxacin and allopurinol. Enzyme inducers (eg rifampicin, carbamazepine and phenytoin) have the opposite effect, but it should be remembered that their discontinuation increases the effect of warfarin. Aspirin and non-steroidal anti-inflammatory drugs (NSAIDs) can increase the risk of bleeding but do not influence the INR.

23   C: Lamotrigine
Sodium valproate is the drug of choice in primary generalised epilepsy, and other effective treatments include phenytoin, carbamazepine, and lamotrigine. Carbamazepine and phenytoin are powerful hepatic enzyme inducers and, therefore, are likely to render the oral contraceptive pill ineffective, and are less appropriate in this situation. Lamotrigine is believed to be free of significant effects on hepatic enzyme activity. Ethosuximide is appropriate for partial rather than generalised epilepsy, particularly absence attacks. Lorazepam raises seizure threshold and is used to treat infantile spasms or epileptiform attacks, including status epilepticus, and is not suitable for long-term prophylaxis of generalised epilepsy.

24   D: Simvastatin 20 mg nocte
The lipid profile suggests modestly elevated total cholesterol and raised triglyceride (TG) concentrations. A number of studies have demonstrated the benefit of 'statin' treatment on cardiovascular morbidity and mortality after myocardial infarction, in patients with raised or 'normal' cholesterol concentrations. Statin treatment lowers total cholesterol and LDL cholesterol, and raises HDL cholesterol concentrations. Statin therapy also lowers TGs: this is thought to be due to the inverse relationship between HDL and TG concentrations, rather than an independent effect. The role of fibrates in reducing cardiovascular risk, by way of lowering TG concentrations after myocardial infarction, has not been established. Dietary intervention alone causes only a modest improvement in lipid profile in most cases, but should be considered alongside drug therapy to enhance the result achieved. Atenolol can increase LDL and lower HDL cholesterol concentrations, but the effect is modest and does not outweigh the important risk reduction achieved by β-blockade.

25   E: Respiratory depression
Paracetamol is the most common drug ingested in overdose situations in the UK. Treatment with *N*-acetylcysteine (NAC) should be instituted if it is suspected that a large amount of paracetamol has been ingested, for example more than 8 g. NAC is instituted where the plasma concentration is above the recommended treatment threshold (eg > 200 mg/l at 4 h). A lower treatment threshold is indicated in patients at risk of liver toxicity: malnourished, anorexic, HIV-positive, patients taking enzyme inducers (phenytoin, carbamazepine, rifampicin, chronic alcohol excess). In acute overdose, paracetamol can cause acute hepatitis, hypoglycaemia due to impaired glycogenolysis, and nausea. Significant respiratory depression strongly suggests concurrent ingestion of opiates (eg as co-proxamol) or, less commonly, benzodiazepines.

26   E: All adverse events for newer drugs should be reported
Only limited information may be available from clinical trials at the time of regulatory submission and licensing of new drugs. Drugs marked with a black triangle in the *British National Formulary* (*BNF*) (▼) are new or licensed for a new indication/route, and all adverse events should be monitored. In other cases, all serious suspected reactions should be reported, even if the causal link is not certain. Unfortunately, there is gross under-reporting of adverse events (less than 10%) in the UK. Some adverse events, including fibrosis or cancer, can be significantly delayed after administration of the suspected causal drug and should still be reported. Adverse events should be reported regardless of whether the use is licensed: this is particularly relevant to paediatric drug use.

27   E: Co-amoxiclav
The biochemical abnormalities are consistent with mechanical biliary obstruction (eg due to gallstones) or cholestasis. Cholestatic jaundice is a complication of a number of drugs, for example co-amoxiclav, erythromycin estolate and chlorpromazine. Other drugs can cause hepatitis, characterised by prominent elevation of ALT, for example isoniazid, hydralazine, rifampicin and paracetamol (usually in overdose). Tetracyclines are an infrequent cause of hepatic steatosis.

28   E: Nephrogenic diabetes insipidus

Chronic lithium treatment disturbs cGMP-mediated effects at both thyroid-stimulating hormone (TSH) and antidiuretic hormone (ADH) receptors, which results in primary hypothyroidism and nephrogenic diabetes insipidus (DI) respectively. Nephrogenic DI causes extracellular volume depletion and total body dehydration, which is likely to account for the majority of the metabolic abnormalities observed. Increased sodium reabsorption at the proximal convoluted tubule is associated with excess lithium reabsorption via a similar mechanism. DI can occur late in the course of lithium treatment, and is a recognised precipitant of lithium toxicity. Bradycardia is a recognised feature of lithium toxicity, and can require temporary pacemaker insertion: in most cases, it does not recur when treatment is recommenced.

29   B: Acute pancreatitis

The rash is indicative of eruptive xanthoma, suggesting underlying hypertriglyceridaemia. Beta-blockers and thiazides both cause increased triglyceride concentrations, and are recognised precipitating factors. The diagnosis would be established by an elevated serum amylase concentration, low calcium and raised triglyceride concentrations. Although the other options appear plausible, acute myocardial infarction is made less likely by normal ECG morphology. Acute hepatitis or gastroenteritis would be less likely to have an abrupt onset, and vomiting is not usually a prominent feature in the presentation of aortic dissection.

30   C: Methanol toxicity

Benzodiazepine and opiate overdose are made unlikely by the high respiratory rate, which is usually depressed in these situations. Metabolic acidosis is a recognised feature of tricyclic antidepressant overdose, but typically pupils are dilated and reflexes may be suppressed or absent. Acute paracetamol overdose is often associated with hypoglycaemia and does not usually cause severe metabolic acidosis. Methanol and ethylene glycol toxicity are typically associated with severe metabolic acidosis, renal tubular acidosis and depressed conscious level. Treatment consists of alcohol administration, to reduce formation of toxic metabolites by hepatic metabolism, and dialysis in certain situations to assist elimination and correct metabolic acidosis.

31   B: Estimated creatinine clearance

The most important consideration is the underlying glomerular filtration rate (GFR), which normally makes the greatest contribution to overall drug clearance. For most drugs, tubular reabsorption and secretion make a comparatively small contribution to overall renal handling. Creatinine clearance, estimated using the Cockcroft–Gault equation, closely approximates to the GFR and may be more accurate than 24-hour urinary creatinine measurements due to incomplete sample collection in many cases. Serum creatinine is less reliable because it is influenced by other factors, for example lean muscle bulk. Height and weight are important general considerations in all prescribing situations, but are less important than GFR in the setting of renal impairment. As a general rule, drugs with high aqueous solubility are heavily dependent on renal clearance, whereas lipid-soluble drugs tend to have greater hepatic clearance. Dose adjustment depending on GFR is independent of the underlying aetiology of the renal impairment.

32   D: Warfarin

The scenario suggests the presence of persistent atrial fibrillation for at least three months. Appropriate investigations include measurement of thyroid function, liver biochemistry, echocardiography (echo) and, in certain cases, measurement of urinary catecholamines. It is important to elicit an alcohol history because this may be an underlying cause of atrial fibrillation, and may make warfarin treatment more hazardous. Warfarin treatment generally reduces the risk of stroke by around one third, and should be titrated to achieve a target INR of 2.0–2.5. It increases the risk of haemorrhagic complications, and the risks of treatment may outweigh the potential benefits (young patients with non-valvular atrial fibrillation, patients who drink alcohol to excess, patients with balance problems or who are prone to falls, those who pursue hazardous pursuits). In the situation presented, attempted cardioversion by amiodarone or DC shock may cause embolism of clots formed within the atria and should not be considered until echo has been performed (transoesophageal is preferred to transthoracic echo in the acute setting). Warfarin treatment for at least six to eight weeks before attempted cardioversion reduces the risk of this potential complication. Aspirin (with or without dipyridamole) has consistently been found to be less effective than warfarin for reducing the risk of thromboembolism in atrial fibrillation.

33   C: Fluoxetine

Fluoxetine and other selective serotonin re-uptake inhibitor (SSRI) antidepressants are commonly implicated as a cause of isolated hyponatraemia. The mechanism is unclear but does not appear to be due to effects on ADH secretion or sensitivity. The background history of psychiatric illness make psychogenic polydipsia an important consideration, but this is less likely given the estimated plasma osmolality, calculated as $([Na^+] + [K^+]) \times 2 + [urea] + [glucose]$, is 282 mosmol/kg (normal reference range 278–298 mosmol/kg). In psychogenic polydipsia and syndrome of inappropriate ADH secretion (SIADH), plasma osmolality is usually low; the two can be distinguished on the basis of urinary osmolality, which is low in the former and inappropriately high in the latter. Discontinuation of the fluoxetine will allow restoration of normal sodium homeostasis and should not be re-introduced. In a significant minority of cases, hyponatraemia will occur in response to alternative SSRIs.

34   B: Dose should be reduced if the trough level is high but peak level satisfactory

In gentamicin prescribing, the dose interval should be determined on the basis of renal clearance, as this is the most important determinant of drug half-life. The peak level should be between 4 and 10 μg/ml, and the target should be towards the upper part of this range in serious infections such as endocarditis. If the peak level is satisfactory but trough levels are high, then the dosing interval should be increased because this suggests drug accumulation, often due to impaired clearance. Furosemide tends to enhance the ototoxic risks of gentamicin treatment, rather than its nephrotoxic properties. Both nephrotoxicity and ototoxicity are recognised complications of gentamicin treatment, even if the peak and trough levels are satisfactory. This is particularly true of treatment prolonged for more than two weeks and is due to tissue accumulation of drug.

35   A: Further studies are required to determine the safety of the drug

All new drugs are intensively monitored for at least one year, and all adverse events should be reported to the local Committee on Safety of Medicines (CSM) using the Yellow Card system. This is important because, to meet the regulatory requirements for licensing application, perhaps only up to 2000 healthy subjects or patients may have received the drug in clinical trials and adverse effects, which may be serious or fatal, occurring with a frequency of 1:1000 or less will not be detected. The fact that the drug is more 'potent' does not imply that the drug is more 'efficacious'. Potency is an expression of drug effect that takes account of dose or concentration. For example, bisoprolol 5 mg daily and atenolol 50 mg daily may be equally efficacious in reducing blood pressure despite the fact that bisoprolol is ten times more potent. In the given scenario, it is also important to consider that treatment to reduce cholesterol is aimed at reducing cardiovascular risk. It cannot be assumed that an equal reduction in cholesterol will lead to an equal reduction in cardiovascular risk, because other drug mechanisms may be important.

36   D: They are implicated in around half of cases of gastric ulceration

NSAIDs are potent inhibitors of cyclo-oxygenase, which reduces the formation of inflammatory cytokines, and they are particularly effective analgesics in the setting of joint or tissue inflammation. However, through the same mechanism, NSAIDs as a class are associated with significant complications and adverse events are reported in as many as 20% of patients. Renal complications include acute tubular necrosis, papillary necrosis and acute renal failure. Gastrointestinal complications are common and include occult gastrointestinal blood loss and peptic ulceration. The adverse gastrointestinal effects are systemic, and seen in animal models where the drugs are given by parenteral administration; enteric-coated preparations therefore do not negate this risk. Through salt and water retention they can aggravate hypertension and congestive heart failure.

37   C: Its absorption might increase up to tenfold if taken with food

The data indicate two important aspects of drug absorption: firstly, the overall systemic drug availability is low and, secondly, there is significant variability in bioavailability. These are unfavourable properties that reduce the prospects for development of an effective oral preparation. If the drug is highly lipid soluble it is more likely to be subject to first-pass metabolism and hepatic clearance, which might account for poor systemic bioavailability. In general, food increases the uptake of lipid-soluble drugs from the gastrointestinal tract, whereas it is more likely to reduce absorption of aqueous drugs. Therefore, food might increase the consistency of drug absorption between individuals or increase bioavailability theoretically up to 100% (a tenfold increase from the data presented in the scenario), although such a dramatic increase would be unusual. The lack of systemic absorption does not imply that the drug would be of no clinical value, as it may be developed as an oral preparation to treat local gastrointestinal infections, or as an intravenous preparation to treat systemic infections (eg vancomycin).

38   D: Slurred speech

Phenytoin is an effective treatment for generalised epilepsy, but is generally less favoured for treatment of younger patients due to its numerous adverse effects, which include gingival hyperplasia, hirsutism, acne and coarseness of facial features. It is a potent hepatic enzyme inducer and, therefore, makes the oral contraceptive pill less effective and women of child-bearing potential should be warned to use alternative birth control methods if appropriate. Due to induced metabolism of vitamin D and folate, osteomalacia and megaloblastic anaemia are recognised complications. More commonly it is associated with a simple macrocytosis and hepatitis. Neurotoxic effects are common, particularly cerebellar toxicity, which may present with unsteady gait, ataxia, nystagmus, slurred speech and incoordination: these effects are more common with high plasma concentrations and therapeutic drug monitoring is important.

39   B: Low molecular weight heparin should be substituted during the first trimester

Specialist referral should be considered, because counselling about risks versus benefits is very important in this situation. Warfarin is a known teratogen and should be discontinued during the first trimester. Its use is associated with increased risk of haemorrhagic complications in the peripartum period and should be monitored closely at this time, or substituted with heparin. Low molecular weight heparin should be used as an alternative during the first trimester because teratogenicity is not a recognised complication. Long-term effects of heparin include thrombocytopenia and osteoporosis.

40   B: Combined preparations may cause malignant melanoma to progress more rapidly

A number of tumours may be oestrogen-dependent, including melanoma, breast carcinoma, hepatoma and desmoid tumours. Progesterone has no significant effect on blood pressure, whereas oestrogen (even in low doses) causes elevation of both systolic and diastolic blood pressure. In some patients, there can be a significant increase in blood pressure, necessitating withdrawal of treatment. The oestrogen component of oral contraceptive preparations increases the risk of arterial and venous thromboembolism. Previous deep vein thrombosis (DVT) may increase the risk of thrombosis related to combined oral contraceptive pill (COCP) preparations; the risk varies between individuals, however, and there may have been an independent precipitant for the first episode, such as orthopaedic trauma. Phenytoin and other anti-epileptic medications are recognised enzyme inducers, which may reduce the effectiveness of both oestrogen and progestogen components of the COCP. Sickle cell crises are not a recognised complication of COCP treatment.

41   C: Bumetanide

In elderly patients, particular caution should be given to drugs in the following classes:

- Diuretics (loop diuretics, thiazide type, potassium-sparing) – due to reduced effectiveness of fluid homeostasis with advancing age, coupled with attenuation of the hypothalamic appreciation of thirst, elderly patients are at greater risk of significant dehydration and intravascular fluid depletion.
- Drugs that impair renal function (NSAIDs, ACE inhibitors, angiotensin-II receptor antagonists) – elderly patients are more prone to the nephrotoxic effects of such drugs due to impaired renal blood flow, and have a greater dependence on the renin-angiotensin-aldosterone system for maintenance of normal glomerular filtration rate.
- Sedative medications (antipsychotic drugs, anxiolytics, especially benzodiazepines, antidepressants) – elderly patients are particularly susceptible to the sedative effects of CNS-active drugs due to loss of cortical tissue, deterioration in blood–brain barrier effectiveness and tissue accumulation in the setting of impaired overall drug clearance.

Renal clearance becomes less effective with advancing age and, therefore, elderly patients are more prone to accumulation of drugs normally subject to renal elimination, such as digoxin.

42   E: The sedative effects are exaggerated by alcohol

Benzodiazepines have anxiolytic and hypnotic properties, which make them suitable for short-term relief of anxiety symptoms and insomnia. Short-acting agents (temazepam, lorazepam and oxazepam) are preferred for insomnia treatment so as to avoid significant morning drowsiness. Additionally, they increase seizure threshold, and diazepam and clonazepam are used for the control of seizures. Long-acting agents (diazepam, chlordiazepoxide) are used for the prevention and treatment of delirium tremens in the setting of acute alcohol withdrawal. Diazepam is a lipid-soluble drug with a wide volume of distribution. In chronic dosing, its half-life ranges from 20 to 90 hours. It has an active metabolite (desmethyldiazepam), which has similar sedative properties and a half-life ranging from 50 to 120 hours. Diazepam and its active metabolite are cleared predominantly by hepatic elimination and treatment is contraindicated in cirrhosis. Benzodiazepines should be used with particular caution in elderly patients, who are more susceptible to the sedative effects. Flumazenil is a specific benzodiazepine antagonist that may be useful for reversing severe respiratory depression. However, it is associated with seizures, especially in patients with existing epilepsy, and should be used with caution. The half-life of flumazenil is significantly shorter than that of diazepam and it should be kept in mind that there may be a relapse of the respiratory depression.

43   D: Metoclopramide is a recognised cause of drug-induced parkinsonism

Metoclopramide and domperidone act through blockade of dopaminergic receptors. They increase lower oesophageal sphincter tone and increase gastric emptying, and are particularly effective for relieving postoperative nausea and for the treatment of gastroparesis in patients with autonomic neuropathy. Domperidone does not significantly cross the blood–brain barrier and drug-induced parkinsonism is a less commonly recognised feature. Cyclizine acts centrally through blockade of cholinergic receptors, and may increase the risk of tachyarrhythmias in the post-MI setting due to vagal withdrawal and relatively high sympathetic cardiac activity. Ondansetron is a 5-hydroxytrptamine (5-HT$_3$) antagonist and possesses powerful anti-emetic properties. Drugs in this class are particularly useful in treating chemotherapy-associated nausea, which often fails to respond to other anti-emetic treatments. They are also effective in treating nausea due to other causes but, predominantly due to their comparatively high cost, are usually restricted to chemotherapy-associated nausea or to patients who have failed to respond to other treatments.

44   B: Erythromycin

In this setting, the commonest causal organisms are staphylococcal and streptococcal bacteria. Prompt treatment is required to prevent development of cellulitis and reduce the risk of local abscess formation. Antimicrobials excreted in breast milk will alter the gastrointestinal flora in the neonate and can cause diarrhoea or gastroenteritis. Penicillins and cephalosporins are excreted in very small quantities and appear generally safe. Tetracyclines are excreted in breast milk and may be taken up into developing bones and teeth of neonates, and are generally avoided; the amount absorbed is probably insignificant, however, because tetracyclines are chelated with calcium in breast milk, thereby limiting their absorption. Metronidazole should be avoided because significant quantities are excreted in breast milk. Sulphonamides should be avoided in mothers nursing babies who are premature, jaundiced or have glucose-6-phosphate dehydrogenase (G6PD) deficiency. Pyridoxine should be given to mother and baby if treatment with isoniazid is required. Trimethoprim, macrolides and vancomycin appear to be safe. Vancomycin would be ineffective as an oral preparation in the given scenario, however.

45   C: Its pharmacological effects should be studied in slow-and-rapid acetylator populations

As a general rule, slow acetylators are more likely to experience good therapeutic effects of the drug but have a greater risk of adverse effects because the circulating drug concentrations are higher. Conversely, rapid acetylators usually derive less benefit from treatment and experience fewer adverse effects due to lower circulating drug concentrations. However, this is not always the case. For example, slow acetylators experience a higher incidence of peripheral neuropathy (direct drug toxicity), whereas rapid acetylators experience a higher incidence of hepatitis (toxicity due to metabolite). Other examples of drugs subject to significant acetylation are procainamide, hydralazine, sulphonamides, sulfasalazine and caffeine. Genetic polymorphisms influence drug effects through pathways other than acetylation, including oxidation phenotype, hydroxylation, G6PD activity and suxamethonium sensitivity. Such polymorphisms are genetically determined and not directly influenced by the coexistence of other diseases. Reflecting their genetic basis, different populations vary: for example, in the UK around half of the population are rapid acetylators, whereas this is the case in more than 90% of Inuits.

RESPIRATORY MEDICINE

46   C: Patients who manifest disease usually have the PiZZ genotype

α_1-AT deficiency is a rare autosomal recessive disorder due to a genetic abnormality affecting chromosome 14. The diagnosis is confirmed by measuring levels of α_1-AT (a protease inhibitor), which are reduced or undetectable. M is the normal allelle. S and Z variants result in decreased production of α_1-AT (S about 60%, Z about 15%). The normal phenotype is PiMM. Patients who manifest disease usually have the PiZZ genotype. Emphysema is the commonest clinical presentation. Liver disease may present as cholestasis in infancy, and there is an increased incidence of hepatocellular carcinoma in adults. Prenatal diagnosis is possible by DNA analysis of chorionic villus samples. Since α_1-AT is an acute phase protein, levels may increase to within the normal range during infections, particularly in heterozygous patients.

α_1-AT deficiency can be treated with synthetic α_1-AT, and supportive management of emphysema and liver disease. Patients should be advised not to smoke as this contributes to the decline in lung function. Liver transplantation should be considered in decompensated cirrhosis, and lung transplantation has been undertaken in some centres.

47   D: Pulmonary hypertension is a commonly recognised feature

The APACHE scoring system is used as an index of disease severity, usually in the Intensive Care Unit (ICU). Daytime somnolence may be assessed using the Epworth scoring system. Obstructive sleep apnoea is characterised by intermittent closure/collapse of the pharyngeal airway, causing apnoeic episodes during sleep, which are terminated when the patient rouses briefly. Patients typically present because of snoring or daytime somnolence. Other features include morning headache, decreased libido, impaired cognitive performance and irritability. The problem is exacerbated by night-time alcohol intake and sedative medication. Patients with obstructive sleep apnoea are usually obese; other predisposing factors are hypothyroidism, acromegaly, large tonsils and retrognathia. Chronic nocturnal hypoxia causes pulmonary vascular constriction, and the condition is often complicated by pulmonary hypertension, and right heart failure (cor pulmonale) in some cases.

Obstructive sleep apnoea is diagnosed by the presence of multiple (typically >15 per hour) hypopnoeic/apnoeic events occurring during the night and resulting in desaturation. This may be established using pulse oximetry and video recording during sleep. Polysomnography may help establish the diagnosis, which involves monitoring of electroencephalogram (EEG), electro-oculogram, electromyogram (EMG), pulse oximetry, airflow at the nose and mouth, thoraco-abdominal movement during sleep, and sometimes video and microphone.

Management includes weight loss advice, avoidance of alcohol and sedatives, and nocturnal CPAP via a nasal mask. Anterior mandibular positioning devices are useful in some patients. Surgical procedures to relieve pharyngeal obstruction may be considered, such as tonsillectomy if enlarged tonsils are thought to be the cause, and tracheostomy in intractable cases. Uvulopalato-pharyngoplasty is not generally helpful. Patients should be told to inform the Driver and Vehicle Licensing Agency (DVLA) and refrain from driving.

48   E: Treatment is based on arterial gas analyses measured when the patient is clinically stable on at least two occasions, three weeks apart

Treatment should be given for at least 15 hours per day to achieve benefit. Two trials in COPD and chronic hypoxia have shown:

- Improved survival (in the MRC study, five-year survival improved from 25% to 41% with 15 hours of oxygen therapy a day)
- Less secondary polycythaemia
- Delayed progression of pulmonary hypertension
- An improvement in neuropsychological health.

Arterial blood gases should be done when the patient is clinically stable and on optimal medical treatment and on at least two occasions, three weeks apart. These should be measured during treatment to ensure that the set flow is achieving an arterial oxygen tension (Pao_2) of > 8 kPa without an unacceptable rise in arterial carbon dioxide tension ($Paco_2$). It is normally provided from an oxygen concentrator via nasal prongs, at a flow rate of 2–4 l/minute.

Patients with COPD who have a Pao_2 of < 7.3 kPa with or without hyper-capnoea, and a forced expiratory volume in one second (FEV_1) of < 1.5 litre should be considered for domiciliary oxygen, or if they have a Pao_2 of 7.3–8.0 kPa and there is evidence of pulmonary hypertension, peripheral oedema or nocturnal hypoxaemia. Continued smoking by the patient or other household members is an absolute contraindication to treatment, due to the fire and explosion hazards. At least six-monthly review is advised.

49   D: Pulmonary embolus

The CO transfer factor is a measure of gas diffusion across the alveolar membrane into capillaries. It is dependent on blood volume, blood flow, surface area of membranes and distribution of ventilation. It is measured by the diffusion of carbon monoxide. The transfer coefficient ($Tlco$) is corrected for lung volume.

Recognised causes of increased CO transfer factor are:

- Pulmonary haemorrhage
- Exercise
- Polycythaemia
- Left-to-right intracardiac shunts
- Asthma.

Recognised causes of decreased CO transfer factor are:

- COPD
- Diffuse interstitial lung disease
- Pneumonia
- Pulmonary oedema
- Pulmonary embolism (acute or chronic)
- Pulmonary hypertension
- Pneumonectomy
- Anaemia
- Arteriovenous malformation

50   D: Increased serum pH
A rise in the pH shifts the haemoglobin-oxygen dissociation curve to the left. An increase in the H^+ ion concentration shifts it to the right. When the curve is shifted to the right, haemoglobin gives up oxygen more readily. This is of physiological importance, for example in acute exercise, where increased local temperature, lactate, $Paco_2$ and decreased pH result in more efficient oxygen delivery to exercising muscle. It is also recognised in chronic hypoxia and chronic anaemia due to increased red blood cell 2,3-diphosphoglycerate (2,3-DPG) concentrations. In transfused packed red cells, there is a significant leftward shift in the oxygen dissociation curve, such that oxygen is bound more avidly to haemoglobin (due to 2,3-DPG depletion and reduced temperature). As a consequence, transfused blood may not improve tissue oxygen delivery for up to 24 hours after administration and can even exacerbate tissue ischaemia in some patients.

51   B: Diazepam overdose
The arterial blood gas pattern is consistent with type II respiratory failure, defined by hypoxia (Pao_2 < 8 kPa) and raised $Paco_2$ (> 6.5 kPa). Type II respiratory failure is caused by alveolar hypoventilation, with or without ventilation-perfusion ($\dot{V}/\dot{Q}$) mismatch.

Recognised causes are:

- Thoracic wall disease, eg kyphoscoliosis, flail chest, ankylosing spondylitis
- Neurological disorders, eg Guillain–Barré, multiple sclerosis, polio, motor neurone disease, cervical cord lesion
- Muscular disease, eg myasthenia gravis, muscular dystrophy
- Sedative drugs, including alcohol intoxication
- Pulmonary disease, eg COPD, late stages of severe asthma, emphysema, pulmonary fibrosis.

The alternative diagnoses are more typically associated with type I respiratory failure, defined by hypoxia (Pao_2 < 8 kPa) and low or normal $Paco_2$. Type I respiratory failure is caused primarily by $\dot{V}/\dot{Q}$ mismatch.

Recognised causes of type I respiratory failure are:

- Pulmonary embolism
- Pneumonia
- Asthma
- Pulmonary oedema
- Pulmonary haemorrhage
- Pneumothorax
- Acute respiratory distress syndrome (ARDS)
- Fibrosing alveolitis
- Emphysema.

52 A: Bacterial pneumonia

Bacterial pneumonia is the most commonly encountered cause of haemoptysis, and is usually accompanied by fever, cough productive of mucopurulent sputum, and pleuritic chest pain.

Other recognised causes of haemoptysis are:

- Bronchogenic cancer
- Bronchiectasis
- Pulmonary TB
- Pulmonary embolism
- Mitral valve disease.

Rarer causes include vascular malformations, mycetoma, connective tissue disease, vasculitis, Goodpasture's syndrome and bleeding diatheses. Mesothelioma is tumour of mesothelial origin that usually occurs in the pleura, and is a late complication of asbestos exposure. Clinical features include chest pain, shortness of breath, weight loss, clubbing and recurrent pleural effusions, but haemoptysis is a rare late complication due to local invasion. Diagnosis is made by typical CT scan appearance and confirmed by histology following a pleural biopsy, and median survival is 12–18 months from diagnosis. Sarcoidosis rarely presents with haemoptysis, which is often secondary to protracted coughing.

53 C: Goodpasture's syndrome

Goodpasture's syndrome is caused by anti-basement membrane antibodies binding the kidney's basement membrane and the alveolar membrane. The antigen involved is within collagen type IV. Proliferative glomerulonephritis and haemoptysis (from pulmonary haemorrhage) result. Infiltrates, particularly in the lower zones, are seen on chest X-ray. Renal biopsy shows crescentic nephritis. Treatment comprises vigorous immunosuppression (usually with steroids and cyclophosphamide) and plasmapheresis. Other diseases that could cause this are systemic lupus erythematosus (SLE) or a systemic vasculitis, such as Wegener's granulomatosis or microscopic polyarteritis.

The history is not typical of Legionnaire's disease, which usually presents with flu-like symptoms preceded by a dry cough and breathlessness. Extra-pulmonary features include diarrhoea and vomiting, hepatitis, renal failure, confusion and coma, and investigations may show lymphopenia, hyponatraemia, deranged liver function tests (LFTs) and haematuria.

54   C: Sarcoidosis
The diagnosis is suggested by the possibility of erythema nodosum, hypercalcaemia and the raised ESR. The chest X-ray is consistent with bilateral hilar lymphadenopathy (BHL) and pulmonary fibrosis, which are typical manifestations of pulmonary sarcoidosis. The disorder has its highest prevalence in young Afro-Caribbean adults. AIDS may cause BHL (either secondary to HIV infection or to opportunistic infection, eg TB). Interstitial changes on chest X-ray may occur secondary to TB, atypical pneumonia or pneumonitis. AIDS often presents with *Pneumocystis carinii* pneumonia (PCP), and patients typically present with breathlessness and hypoxia despite relatively normal chest X-ray appearances. Deranged liver function tests, lymphopenia, and raised ESR are recognised features of AIDS, but hypercalcaemia is not.

TB can present with cough, breathlessness and malaise, and may be associated with erythema nodosum and raised ESR. However, pulmonary TB rarely presents with features of arthralgia and hypercalcaemia.

SLE can cause bilateral interstitial shadowing on chest X-ray due to recurrent pneumonitis and pulmonary fibrosis; hilar lymphadenopathy is uncommon.

Pulmonary lymphoma is most commonly associated with underlying chronic lymphocytic leukaemia and is uncommon in patients under 60 years old. It can present with malaise, shortness of breath and recurrent pneumonia. Most patients are found to have peripheral lymphadenopathy and/or systemic symptoms.

**55   C: Neuro-ophthalmic involvement necessitates steroid
        treatment**
Sarcoidosis is a multisystem non-caseating granulomatous disease of unknown cause that mainly affects young adults (aged 20–40 years), and Afro-Caribbeans are more commonly affected. Sarcoidosis may be asymptomatic. Recognised features are erythema nodosum, bilateral hilar lymphadenopathy and/or polyarthralgia. Respiratory symptoms include dry cough, progressive shortness of breath and reduced exercise tolerance; the chest X-ray is abnormal in 90% of patients due to hilar lymphadenopathy, pulmonary infiltration and fibrosis.

Extrapulmonary manifestations include:

1. Eyes:
   - anterior uveitis
2. Skin:
   - erythema nodosum
   - lupus pernio
3. CNS:
   - space-occupying lesion
   - optic neuritis
   - meningitis
   - peripheral neuropathy
   - mononeuritis multiplex
   - neuropsychiatric illness
4. Bone:
   - arthritis
   - cysts
5. Haematological:
   - lymphadenopathy
   - splenomegaly
6. Cardiovascular:
   - cardiomyopathy
   - arrhythmias
   - complete heart block
7. Renal:
   - interstitial nephritis
8. Salivary glands:
   - enlargement of parotid and lacrimal glands.

Blood tests may reveal a raised ESR, lymphopenia, abnormal LFTs, raised serum angiotensin converting enzyme (ACE), immunoglobulins and Ca^{2+}. Pulmonary function tests may be normal or show reduced lung volumes, reduced transfer factor and a restrictive deficit. Tissue biopsy is diagnostic and shows non-caseating granulomata. Bronchoalveolar lavage reveals increased lymphocytes in active disease and increased neutrophils with pulmonary fibrosis. The Kveim test is positive in about 75% of patients but is virtually obsolete.

Most patients do not require specific treatment, but corticosteroids are indicated in:

- Neuro-ophthalmic disease
- Parenchymal lung disease
- Cardiac involvement
- Hypercalcaemia.

In severe cases, immunosuppressant therapy may be of benefit, (eg methotrexate, azathioprine, cyclophosphamide).

56 A: Churg–Strauss syndrome

This patient has multisystem disease involving the respiratory system and skin. There is an eosinophilia, anaemia and raised ESR, and evidence of pulmonary infiltrates/haemorrhage. This suggests a vasculitis (namely polyarteritis nodosa or Churg–Strauss syndrome). The history of asthma symptoms and positive pANCA is strongly suggestive of Churg–Strauss syndrome.

Extrinsic allergic alveolitis is a hypersensitivity pneumonitis caused by IgG-mediated type III and IV hypersensitivity to inhaled organic dust. Examples include farmer's lung, bird fancier's lung and mushroom worker's lung. Patients present with fever, cough and shortness of breath four to nine hours after exposure. Symptoms usually settle within 48 hours. Chest X-ray may be normal or show nodular shadows and hazy infiltrates. Prolonged cases are associated with development of fibrosing alveolitis.

Wegener's granulomatosis is a vasculitis of small/medium-sized arteries. It is characterised by respiratory tract involvement, pulmonary disease and glomerulonephritis. It is not associated with eosinophilia or asthma. cANCA is positive in around 90% of cases.

Goodpasture's syndrome is a pulmonary-renal disease caused by binding of antibody to glomerular and alveolar basement membrane. Patients often present with haemoptysis, shortness of breath, pulmonary haemorrhage and haematuria, and it is generally not associated with eosinophilia, rash or pANCA.

57 E: Rheumatoid arthritis

Rheumatoid arthritis is associated with a pleural effusion that is typically associated with a low glucose concentration (< 2 mmol/l) and C4 complement (< 0.04 g/l), and the following features of an exudate: high total protein concentration (> 30 g/l) and lactate dehydrogenase (LDH) concentration (> 250 U/l). Recognised causes of pleural exudates are:

- Malignancy
- Parapneumonic effusion
- Pulmonary infarction
- Rheumatoid arthritis
- AIDS
- Benign asbestos effusion
- Pancreatitis
- Post-MI syndrome
- Yellow nail syndrome
- Drugs, eg methotrexate, amiodarone, phenytoin.

Pleural transudates (typically associated with total protein < 30 g/l and LDH < 250 U/l) are caused by:

- Left ventricular failure
- Liver cirrhosis
- Hypoalbuminaemia
- Peritoneal dialysis
- Hypothyroidism
- Nephrotic syndrome
- Mitral stenosis
- Pulmonary embolus
- Constrictive pericarditis
- Superior vena cava obstruction
- Ovarian hyperstimulation
- Meigs' syndrome.

58   C: It is inherited in an autosomal recessive manner with a prevalence of 1 in 2500

The principal abnormality involves chloride channel function, such that intraluminal secretions are highly viscid. An abnormality of the chloride ion channel is found on chromosome 7 in most cases (the cystic fibrosis transmembrane conductance regulator, *CFTR*, gene). Genetic testing can confirm the diagnosis, and in most patients sweat testing identifies an abnormally high sodium concentration (> 60 mmol/l). Clinical manifestations are principally due to impaired ciliary movement, including recurrent respiratory infections, infertility in both males and females, and pancreatitis and diabetes mellitus are well recognised complications. Amyloidosis is a recognised long-term complication due to recurrent inflammation and infective complications of the disease.

59   E: Bronchiectasis is associated with defective humoral immunity

The hallmark feature of bronchiectasis is permanent dilatation of small airways, and it is typically associated with recurrent pulmonary infection. Chest X-ray may be normal or show ring, tramline or tubular shadows. Pulmonary function tests can demonstrate a restrictive or obstructive pattern, or a combination of both, and CO transfer is usually impaired to some extent. High-resolution CT scanning is the diagnostic method of choice (> 90% sensitivity). There are a number of recognised causes:

Congenital:

- Selective IgA deficiency
- Kartagener's syndrome – ciliary dyskinesis associated with infertility, dextrocardia and situs inversus
- Primary immotile cilia syndrome
- X-linked hypogammaglobulinaemia.

Acquired:

- Childhood pneumonia, whooping cough, measles
- Post-TB
- Allergic bronchopulmonary aspergillosis
- Distal to obstructed bronchus (foreign body, tumour)
- Associated with pulmonary fibrosis and sarcoidosis
- Idiopathic
- Immune deficiency, eg chronic lymphocytic leukaemia (CLL) in adults, acute lymphoblastic leukaemia (ALL) in children.

60   C: Response to isoniazid is determined by genetic variation
Isoniazid is metabolised principally by acetylation. Acetylator status is subject to genetic polymorphism. Slow acetylators are exposed to higher drug concentrations and have a better therapeutic response, while rapid acetylators have a poorer response and higher relapse rate. Isoniazid, pyrazinamide and rifampicin are recognised causes of hepatitis. Rifampicin typically causes red discoloration of tears, nasal secretions and urine. Peripheral neuropathy is a well-recognised adverse effect of isoniazid therapy, particularly with high doses; treatment with pyridoxine reduces the risks of this complication. A specific adverse effect of ethambutol is retrobulbar neuritis, which is more common with high doses and prolonged treatment. Early ophthalmology review and drug discontinuation are advised in the event of any deterioration in vision, and regular fundoscopy is recommended.

61   E: There is a recognised association with Marfan's syndrome
In the acute phase, a moderate to large pneumothorax is associated with hypoxia due to shunting of blood through the collapsed lung. However, there is progressive redistribution of blood flow and the patient with otherwise 'healthy' lungs is able to correct hypoxia. Pulmonary function tests often show a restrictive lung defect and reduction of vital capacity. Pneumothorax may occur in a number of inherited collagen disorders, such as Marfan's syndrome, Ehlers–Danlos syndrome and pseudoxanthoma elasticum. High lung inflation pressures can predispose to pneumothorax among patients receiving intermittent positive pressure ventilation (IPPV). There is a recognised association between cavitating lung disease (eg tuberculosis), where a subpleural cavity ruptures into the pleural space. Spontaneous pneumothorax in young patients, in the absence of an underlying cause, is most common in those of a tall, lean constitution. Recurrent pneumothorax occurs only in a minority of such patients.

62   B: It is a recognised feature of obstructive sleep apnoea
Pulmonary hypertension is typically associated with systolic and mean pulmonary pressures above 30 and 15 mmHg respectively. The commonest cause is chronic obstructive airways disease (as a feature of cor pulmonale). Other causes include recurrent pulmonary embolism, primary pulmonary hypertension, and hypoxic pulmonary hypertension as seen in obstructive sleep apnoea. Rarer causes include schistosomiasis, which is associated with obliteration of small pulmonary arteries. Pulmonary hypertension can be associated with a loud (or even palpable) pulmonary component of the second heart sound due to valve closure under increased pressure. In long-standing cases there may be right heart failure, associated with raised JVP, hepatomegaly and peripheral oedema. Cannon *a* waves are a feature of atrial contraction against a closed tricuspid valve and are characteristically found in complete atrioventricular heart block or nodal rhythms.

63   D: The right hemidiaphragm can be elevated compared to the left side
The right hemidiaphragm is often elevated compared to the left, although in 10–15% of normal PA films both are of equal height. The normal landmark for the right hemidiaphragm on an inspiratory PA film is the level of the 6th rib. In a normal chest X-ray, the trachea is often deviated slightly to the right. The normal heart width is less than 50% of the maximum horizontal thoracic diameter (the cardiothoracic ratio), and heart size varies by up to 1 cm between systole and diastole during the cardiac cycle; in some cases, there may be a thin silhouette outlining the cardiac border due to movement artefact. The carina normally overlies the 4th to 5th thoracic vertebrae.

64   B: Fixed wide carina seen during bronchoscopy
An FEV_1 of less than 2.0 litres, or less than 50% predicted, would indicate inadequate pulmonary reserve to allow pneumonectomy. The left recurrent laryngeal nerve runs an intrathoracic course and is often affected by local tumour infiltration; however, the right recurrent laryngeal nerve only descends as far as the right subclavian artery and infiltration is unusual. Another cause for right recurrent laryngeal nerve involvement should be sought before the patient is declared inoperable. A fixed wide carina suggests significant mediastinal metastases and, as for lesions within 1 cm of the carina, such tumours are usually considered inoperable. Although hypercalcaemia might suggest multiple bony metastases (which would render the primary lesion inoperable), it is often a paraneoplastic complication of squamous cell carcinoma. Haemoptysis can be a feature of direct tumour invasion or a feature of coexistent pneumonia or repetitive coughing.

65   C: Emphysema
Common causes of obstructive lung disease include asthma, chronic bronchitis and emphysema. Options A, B, D and E are recognised causes of restrictive lung disease, characterised by impaired lung compliance. Pulmonary compliance is an index of how easily the lung (and/or chest wall) may be stretched between inspiration and expiration. Reduction of overall alveolar tissue, as occurs in emphysema, causes less resistance to stretch and, therefore, increases pulmonary compliance.

NEUROLOGY

66   A: Benign intracranial hypertension
Headache that is worst in the mornings or exacerbated by straining or postural change is typical of that associated with raised intracranial pressure. Benign intracranial hypertension is more common in female patients, typically presenting between 20 and 40 years of age. It is typically associated with a normal CT brain appearance and intracranial pressure (ICP) > 30 cm. Retinoids and tetracyclines, as used for acne treatment, have been implicated as a cause in some cases. Around half of patients experience some degree of visual loss, which is severe in 5–10% of cases. Acetazolamide and loop diuretics are effective treatments, but cerebrospinal fluid (CSF) drain insertion may be required in some cases. In the majority of cases, meningioma, craniopharyngioma and syringomyelia will be associated with predominantly peripheral neurological signs. Tuberculous meningitis can be associated with raised intracranial pressure as a late feature.

67   B: Graves' disease
Graves' disease is an autoimmune disorder characterised by ophthalmopathy, retro-orbital swelling due to soft-tissue inflammation, pretibial myxoedema and thyroid dysfunction. High resting pulse rate is suggestive of hyperthyroidism, which is a common feature of early thyroid involvement, whereas hypothyroidism is a more common manifestation of later stages of the disease. Proptosis is often asymmetrical, and may be worsened by cigarette smoke. Cavernous sinus thrombosis often causes a painful, suffused orbit and periorbital tissue, and may be provoked by localised infection. Retro-orbital lymphoma typically causes unilateral proptosis, but is a very uncommon condition.

68   D: Sagittal sinus thrombosis
The prominent feature of the CSF examination is the raised protein concentration, which could be caused by acoustic neuroma, sarcoidosis, spinal cord blockade (Froin's syndrome), sagittal sinus thrombosis or Guillain–Barré syndrome. The presentation with headache makes answer D more likely. Sagittal sinus thrombosis is often associated with a normal CT head appearance, and the diagnosis is often established by MRI scanning or magnetic resonance angiography. Viral meningitis is typically associated with a higher lymphocyte count. Guillain–Barré syndrome and meningioma are typically associated with peripheral neurological features, and headache is a less prominent feature.

69   B: Co-amoxiclav

The clinical scenario suggests worsening respiratory function, which is strongly suggestive of declining control of her underlying myasthenia gravis. Appropriate investigations include forced vital capacity (FVC) and arterial blood gas analysis, looking for increased $Paco_2$ as evidence of hypoventilation. Early discussion with the Intensive Care Department is important because this clinical condition can deteriorate rapidly, and invasive ventilatory support may be required. There are a number of recognised causes of acute deterioration of myasthenia gravis, including inadvertent omission of the usual medication, sepsis, pregnancy, thyrotoxicosis, hypokalaemia, and a number of drugs. The latter includes antibiotics, propranolol, lidocaine, and D-penicillamine. In this particular scenario, it is possible that the underlying pyelonephritis and sepsis or the co-amoxiclav treatment might have precipitated her symptoms. However, the temporal relationship between deteriorating lung function and antibiotic treatment make this the most likely explanation.

70   B: Factor V Leiden mutation is a recognised cause of increased stroke risk

Haematological investigations should be considered in all patients under 50 who present with stroke. This should include full blood count, ESR and plasma viscosity. Other tests, which may require referral to a specialist centre, are protein C and protein S concentrations, antithrombin III, lupus anticoagulant, anticardiolipin antibody, factor V Leiden mutation (activated protein C resistance) and haemoglobin electrophoresis. Lupus anticoagulant and anticardiolipin antibodies are found in SLE and in antiphospholipid syndrome. Anticardiolipin antibodies are also present in patients with other autoimmune diseases, HIV infection, and in association with any one of a number of drug treatments, including phenytoin, valproate and hydralazine.

Factor V Leiden mutation is the most commonly inherited pro-thrombotic state, which results in functional resistance to activated protein C despite normal protein C concentrations. The combined oral contraceptive pill is responsible for around one in eight strokes in women aged 20–45 years, and these are even more likely in the presence of coexistent hypertension and smoking. Other important haematological causes of stroke include myeloproliferative disorders, polycythaemia rubra vera, essential thrombocythaemia and intravascular B-cell lymphoma.

Antiphospholipid antibody syndrome is characteristically associated with thrombocytopenia due to cross-reactive antibody formation.

71 A: Bacterial meningitis

The initial presentation is suggestive of basal skull fracture giving rise to CSF rhinorrhoea, despite the normal skull X-ray appearances. This might have been confirmed by CT head scan and finding glucose in the nasal secretions at the time of the initial presentation. Bacterial meningitis is a recognised feature of basal skull fracture. Intracranial haemorrhage is likely to present with focal neurological signs, and the temporal relation makes subarachnoid haemorrhage unlikely. The most commonly implicated pathogens are *Streptococcus pneumoniae* and meningococcal bacteria. Appropriate investigations include CT head and CSF microscopy and culture and analysis for protein and glucose. Treatment with high-dose intravenous cephalosporin should be administered as soon as the diagnosis is suspected, while awaiting confirmation of the diagnosis.

72 B: Brown-Séquard syndrome

The features are consistent with partial cord hemisection in the cervical region, which is characterised by ipsilateral pyramidal tract (upper motor neurone) disturbance below the level of the lesion (pyramidal-distribution weakness, brisk reflexes and upgoing plantar response), ipsilateral interruption of the dorsal columns (vibration and joint-position sense) and contralateral spinothalamic tract disturbance (pain and temperature sensation). The progressive history in the clinical scenario make disc prolapse a less likely alternative diagnosis, and spinal artery stenosis very unlikely. Syringomyelia typically presents with upper motor neurone features affecting both lower limbs, and lower motor neurone features (pyramidal-distribution weakness, flaccidity and reduced or absent reflexes) in the upper limbs.

73 E: Endarterectomy is indicated if right carotid artery stenosis is > 80%

The relationship between bruits and stenoses is not simple, and their presence does not discriminate between mild and severe stenoses. They should not be relied upon to detect significant stenosis as there is a high false-negative rate, and duplex scanning should be performed in all cases of stroke or transient ischaemic attack (TIA) in a carotid artery distribution. Endarterectomy is a complex procedure associated with high immediate complication rates, typically around 5% for major stroke or death. Therefore, the procedure is only contemplated in cases where there is consistency between the clinical presentation and stenosis (symptomatic stenosis), and in those cases where the risk of future stroke is particularly high (stenosis >70%). In a man of this age, a first TIA would herald an annual stroke risk of 5–10%, depending on the presence of other major risk factors.

74   E: Vasospasm is a major cause of morbidity
Arterial vasospasm is an important complication, and outcome has been significantly improved by the administration of nimodipine, a dihydropyridine calcium-channel blocker. A further complication is obstructive hydrocephalus, which is present in up to 20% of cases within the first two weeks. CT scanning identifies blood in around 90% of cases within the first week, with the highest yield close to the time of symptom onset. Therefore, a negative scan does not exclude the diagnosis. Other diagnostic features include bloodstained CSF and the presence of xanthochromasia. However, lumbar puncture carries a significant risk of coning and should be avoided if possible. Untreated sub-arachnoid haemorrhage (SAH) carries a mortality rate of approximately 45% within the first eight weeks, and re-bleeding makes a significant contribution (occurs in around 30–40% within the first two weeks). Around 10% of patients bleed from an angioma, 15–20% from multiple aneurysms. In around 25% of cases the source of bleeding is not identified, even at autopsy.

75   A: Impaired upward gaze is a recognised feature of Parkinson's disease
In both Parkinson's disease and Huntington's chorea, upward gaze can be affected. Eye movement disorders, including oculogyric crises, are characteristic of postencephalitic parkinsonism. Centres for voluntary fixation are located in both frontal lobes. If the frontal lobe is stimulated (eg epilepsy) the eyes turn away from that side, and if damaged (eg cortical stroke) the eyes turn towards the lesion and, hence, away from the hemiparetic side. The pathways descend and cross within the midbrain and the brainstem. A stroke affecting the brainstem can therefore cause the opposite effect to that seen in a cortical stroke, such that the gaze is towards the hemiparetic side.

In progressive supranuclear palsy (Steele–Richardson–Olszewski syndrome) voluntary downward gaze is typically severely impaired; as the disorder progresses, gaze in all directions may become affected.

76   A   CSF oligoclonal bands are a recognised feature of SLE
CSF protein is derived from filtration of serum across the bloodbrain barrier, from the cellular components of CSF, and from brain interstitial fluid. In conditions where the bloodbrain barrier breaks down (eg meningitis) the CSF protein content rises due to leakage of plasma albumin and other proteins. In such cases, the globulin component and globulin:albumin ratio remains low.

Excess production of intrathecal immunoglobulins, as part of an immune response, results in an increased globulin fraction. An oligoclonal gamma-globulin band will be detected in the CSF electrophoresis (usually IgG). An oligoclonal immune response is a characteristic finding in established multiple sclerosis, but is present in only 50% of patients at the time of diagnosis, increasing as the disease progresses. Diagnosis is based on a consistent clinical history, white matter changes identified on MRI scanning and impaired nerve conduction (eg auditory-evoked responses). Oligoclonal bands are also found in up to 10% of healthy individuals and do not appear to be of pathological consequence. Therefore, oligoclonal bands alone offer neither a sensitive nor a specific diagnostic test for multiple sclerosis (MS). Other conditions that may give rise to oligoclonal CSF bands are sarcoidosis, SLE, Guillain–Barré syndrome, subacute sclerosing panencephalitis (SSPE), meningitis, encephalitis and CNS tumours.

A monoclonal antibody may appear in the CSF of patients with multiple myeloma, lymphoma or benign paraproteinaemia. If the CNS is involved the protein may occur in larger quantities than in plasma.

77   C: Impaired red-green colour vision is a recognised feature
The diagnosis of MS is predominantly a clinical one based on temporally and anatomically discrete neurological lesions. Investigations aid diagnosis but each is associated with a significant rate of false-negative reporting. MRI scanning is the diagnostic modality of choice and demonstrates white matter changes; recent plaques enhance with gadolinium. Auditory- and visual-evoked responses are often abnormal, even in the absence of a history suggesting optic neuritis. CSF examination may demonstrate oligoclonal bands in around half of patients at the time of initial diagnosis. Impaired red-green colour discrimination is a common finding, as a feature of previous or subclinical optic neuritis.

Male sex, onset > 40 years, predominantly motor signs at presentation, poor recovery between relapses, and short relapse intervals are all poor prognostic indicators. Corticosteroids do not reduce the risk of future relapses, and do not improve functional recovery during an acute relapse. Short courses of high-dose corticosteroids (eg intravenous methylprednisolone) appear to be effective in reducing the duration of acute relapse. Interferon α and interferon β appear to be effective in reducing relapse risk in selected patients, but their effectiveness in wider patient groups has not been confirmed.

78   B: Impaired joint-position sense is a characteristic feature
SCDC is a neurological manifestation of vitamin B_{12} deficiency, which is usually (but not always) accompanied by a megaloblastic anaemia or macrocytosis. The principal damage occurs in the dorsal root ganglia and posterior columns, and typically the thoracic cord is most heavily involved. Typically, patients present with features of a peripheral neuropathy, with loss of joint-position and vibration senses, and absent plantar responses. In advanced cases there is subsequent involvement of the corticospinal tracts, causing motor signs in the lower limbs. Other recognised features include mild fever and, in severe cases, dementia and visual disturbance due to optic neuropathy. The upper limbs are only involved in very severe cases as the disease progresses. Vitamin B_{12} administration can delay any further progression, but recovery is often only partial and it is better if treatment is commenced promptly.

**79   C: Multi-infarct dementia is more common in patients with
        type 2 diabetes**

It is extremely difficult to distinguish between multi-infarct dementia and
Alzheimer's disease, despite detailed clinical assessment and radiological
assessment with CT, MRI and functional positron emission tomography (PET)
scanning. The incidence of multi-infarct aetiology is around 10–30% of cases,
and the majority are due to Alzheimer's disease. Classically, multi-infarct
dementia causes a stepwise clinical deterioration, whereas patients with
Alzheimer's disease suffer a progressive clinical decline and the diagnosis may
become clearer over a period of prolonged observation. Multi-infarct dementia
is much more common in patients with established cerebrovascular disease and
in those with major cardiovascular risk factors, especially diabetes. Gait
disturbance and urinary incontinence are findings that raise clinical suspicion of
normal-pressure hydrocephalus. In dementia of either aetiology, short-term
memory is often more prominently affected than long-term memory (which can
be preserved until late in the disease course). Extrapyramidal clinical signs
raise the possibility of parkinsonism, Wilson's disease or Huntingdon's chorea.
Particularly severe behavioural disturbance might suggest Pick's disease, a rare
form of dementia characterised by focal frontal and temporal atrophy.

**80   A: Downward nystagmus is characteristic of lesions at the
        level of the foramen magnum**

Nystagmus is described according to the direction of the fast phase of eye
movement. The amplitude of nystagmus is greatest when looking in the
direction of the fast movement. In peripheral lesions, the direction of the
nystagmus is away from the side of the lesion, whereas in central lesions it is
towards the lesion. Only occasionally are patients aware of the abnormal ocular
movements (especially if of sudden onset). In ataxic nystagmus, the abducting
eye moves laterally with coarse nystagmus; the other eye fails to adduct and
may show fine nystagmus. The site of the lesion is the median longitudinal
fasciculus, which communicates between the fourth cranial nerve (leading eye)
and the third cranial nerve (following eye). It is almost pathognomonic of
multiple sclerosis, but is a recognised complication of diabetes mellitus, CNS
tumours and encephalitis. Benign positional vertigo induces nystagmus in a
horizontal plane only, and can be reproduced when the head is turned suddenly
when the patient is supine with head extended (the Hallpike manoeuvre).

81   D: Local phenol injections are associated with clinical improvement

Phenol injections have been used to destroy dorsal root ganglia in the appropriate location, which has led to improvement in some patients. Other treatments include diazepam, baclofen and dantrolene sodium. All of these treatments are associated with muscle weakness, however, and the risks and benefits of treatment require careful consideration on an individual basis. Baclofen is believed to promote γ-aminobutyric acid (GABA), an inhibitory neurotransmitter, at the spinal cord level. It is neurotoxic, and can causes confusion, hypotonia, fatigue, drowsiness and respiratory depression, necessitating ventilatory support in certain cases. Topical applications are ineffective. Intrathecal administration has been successful in selected patients, but is associated with a high rate of complications and undertaken only in a minority of patients under specialist inpatient supervision. Dantrolene treatment inhibits release of calcium from the sarcoplasmic reticulum, thereby causing dissociation of excitation-contraction coupling. Its major adverse effect is hepatotoxicity, which is more likely in the presence of existing liver disease, and recognised adverse effects are acute hepatitis, chronic active hepatitis and cirrhosis.

82   B: Guillain–Barré syndrome

Guillain–Barré syndrome is an immune-mediated acute demyelinating polyneuropathy that typically presents one to four weeks after acute infection (most commonly respiratory or gastrointestinal infection). Limb, abdominal and back pain can be the first symptom. Typically, there is progressive weakness that extends from the peripheries to central muscle groups. Ventilatory support may be required in some cases. Steroid treatment is ineffective, but plasma exchange and intravenous immunoglobulin administration are effective in some patients. The majority of patients make a complete neurological recovery, but symptoms or signs persist in 10–15% of patients. There is an early mortality rate of 2–5% due to hypoventilation and infective or thrombotic complications. Thoracic vertebral collapse would not account for the abnormal symptoms in the upper limbs, and subacute combined degeneration of the cord typically manifests with posterior column features (impaired vibration and joint-position senses), with motor involvement as a later feature.

83   C: Oral prednisolone may speed recovery from Bell's palsy

Bell's palsy is an idiopathic condition that affects both sexes at all ages. The site of damage is believed to be the portion of the facial nerve within the facial canal, resulting in a lower motor neurone pattern of facial weakness. Ipsilateral involvement of the chorda tympani and the nerve to stapedius can cause impaired taste and hyperacusis respectively. Patients often complain of pain around the ear preceding the onset of facial weakness, and may complain of facial numbness despite the lack of objective clinical signs of impaired sensation. Vesicles on the ear or palate indicate that the lower motor neurone weakness is caused by herpes zoster, rather than Bell's palsy. In contrast, facial weakness that accompanies acute stroke or transient ischaemic attacks is less extensive. There is bilateral upper motor neurone supply to each lower motor neurone of the seventh cranial nerve so that there is preservation, at least in part, of the frontalis muscle and patients retain the ability to wrinkle the forehead on both sides. There is spontaneous recovery in around 75% of cases within 2–12 weeks, and corticosteroids may hasten recovery. Aberrant neural repair can lead to unwanted facial movements or inappropriate tearing or salivation on the affected side.

84   B: Acute viral meningitis due to enterovirus infection

Viral infection is the most common cause of meningitis, caused by enterovirus (echovirus, coxsackievirus or polio), mumps, influenza, herpes simplex, varicella zoster, Epstein–Barr or HIV. Enterovirus infection is the most commonly identified cause, and is often associated with a blanching erythematous rash. CSF typically shows a lymphocytosis (10–2000 cells/mm^3) with normal protein and glucose concentrations. In many cases, headache is improved by lumbar puncture, suggesting that it is mediated at least in part by a small increase in CSF pressure. There is no specific treatment, and the condition is benign and self-limiting. In both tuberculous and malignant meningitis, glucose concentrations are typically low and protein concentrations elevated. Bacterial meningitis is typically associated with a reduced glucose concentration and CSF microscopy shows increased neutrophils ± lymphocytes; Gram stain often identifies the presence of bacterial pathogens.

85   E: Thoracic spinalcord compression

The frontal lobes contain micturition centres, which are linked to the key micturition centre in the pons. Parasympathetic fibres pass from the pons via the lateral columns (bilateral supply) to emerge at S2–4. Sympathetic fibres leave the lumbar spinal cord to synapse in the inferior hypogastric plexus. A number of conditions disturb normal bladder function:

- Atonic bladder (lower motor neurone lesion), eg sacral cord or nerve root lesions. This gives rise to loss of detrusor contraction and difficulty commencing micturition, and results in bladder distension and overflow.
- Hypertonic bladder (upper motor neurone lesion), eg pyramidal tract lesion in the cord or brainstem. This results in urgency, frequency, urge incontinence, incomplete bladder emptying due to incoordination between bladder contraction and sphincter relaxation.
- Cortical, eg frontal lesion. This results in loss of awareness of bladder fullness, difficulty initiating micturition, inappropriate or antisocial micturition.

The symptoms described in this scenario are suggestive of an upper motor neurone lesion, such as external thoracic cord compression, which is likely to be associated with a spastic paraparesis. Anticholinergics (oxybutynin or imipramine), baclofen and intermittent self-catheterisation may offer effective relief of symptoms.

86   D: Levodopa is a recognised cause of postural hypotension

Levodopa (L-dopa) is a precursor to dopamine that is able to cross the blood–brain barrier. It is usually given in combination with a peripheral dopa-decarboxylase inhibitor (eg carbidopa, which does not cross the blood–brain barrier) to prevent conversion to dopamine in the peripheries. This has the dual effect of reducing the peripheral adverse effects of dopamine (flushing, hypotension) and enhancing the amount of L-dopa available to cross the blood–brain barrier. Carbidopa alone is ineffective. Postural hypotension is a well recognised adverse effect of L-dopa treatment, and should not be confused with autonomic neuropathy features that occur in Shy–Drager syndrome. L-dopa treatment is complicated by the development of 'end of dose deterioration' and 'on-off' effects, which can partly be overcome by more frequent administration of divided doses. Early initiation of treatment is likely to be associated with earlier onset of 'on-off' phenomena, but the risk of this adverse event occurring is not increased. Tolcapone is a catechol-*O*-methyltransferase inhibitor, which reduces the motor fluctuations seen with L-dopa; its use allows less frequent administration of L-dopa. Anticholinergic treatment (eg benzhexol and benztropine) is effective in controlling tremor and rigidity, but is notoriously ineffective for treatment of bradykinesia.

87   B: Amyotrophic lateral sclerosis

The combination of muscle wasting and brisk reflexes is very highly suggestive of motor neurone disease (MND). MND typically presents with a combination of upper and lower motor neurone features, usually after 50 years age and more often in men than in women. Cognitive and sensory functions remain intact. The clinical course is progressive decline, and the mean time from diagnosis to death is around one year, often due to respiratory failure or infective complications. There is no established effective treatment, although glutamate antagonists appear to offer some benefits in some patients (eg riluzole). Patients may require extensive input from speech therapists and physiotherapists, and nutritional support via percutaneous gastrostomy is often required. Common patterns of involvement are:

- Progressive muscular atrophy: weakness and wasting of distal limb muscles, fasciculation, diminished or absent reflexes.
- Amyotrophic lateral sclerosis: proximal and distal muscle wasting and weakness with fasciculation, spasticity with exaggerated reflexes and extensor plantars. Pyramidal tract features typically predominate. Bulbar and pseudobulbar palsy are late features.
- Progressive bulbar palsy: early tongue, palate and pharyngeal involvement. Tongue wasting and fasciculation, dysarthria and dysphagia.

88   C: Hyperkalaemia
The clinical scenario is suggestive of proximal myopathy. This is a recognised feature of a number of endocrine and metabolic disorders, and rarely has a primarily neurological cause. Causes include hypokalaemia, hypercalcaemia, hypocalcaemia, hyper- or hypothyroidism, Cushing's syndrome, Addison's disease and alcohol excess. Hypo- or hyperkalaemia can occur in familial periodic paralyses, which are characterised by prolonged profound weakness that may be precipitated by physical exertion or eating. A number of drugs are recognised causes of proximal muscle weakness, including thiazide diuretics, corticosteroids, carbenoxolone and acetylcholinesterase (ACE) inhibitors.

89   C: Eaton–Lambert syndrome
Eaton–Lambert syndrome is a paraneoplastic disorder characterised by weakness of proximal limb muscles, easy fatiguability and diminished reflexes. It is most commonly associated with underlying small-cell lung carcinoma, and the presence of anti-calcium channel antibodies confirms the diagnosis. Interestingly, the neurological features often present before the diagnosis of lung cancer has been established. The key differential diagnoses are myasthenia gravis and Guillain–Barré syndrome; however, in these disorders the weakness tends to spread from distal to proximal muscle groups. Nerve conduction studies and electromyography can help to distinguish these alternative diagnoses. In some cases, treatment of the underlying malignancy has resulted in neurological improvement. Immunoglobulin administration is associated with clinical improvement in some patients.

ENDOCRINOLOGY

90   D: Metoclopramide

Galactorrhoea arises in the setting of hyperprolactinaemia. Prolactin is released from the pituitary under negative control by dopamine from the hypothalamus. Therefore, dopaminergic agonists, such as L-dopa or bromocriptine, will reduce prolactin release. Dopamine antagonists that cross the blood–brain barrier, such as metoclopramide, increase prolactin release.

Other causes of hyperprolactinaemia and/or galactorrhoea are:

- Pregnancy
- Acute stress, eg epileptic seizure
- Oestrogens
- Phenothiazines
- Damage to the hypothalamus or pituitary stalk, eg by radiation or tumour
- Renal or hepatic failure
- Nipple stimulation
- Polycystic ovarian syndrome.

91   E: Primary adrenal insufficiency

Chronic primary adrenal insufficiency may present with anorexia and weight loss, fatigue, generalised weakness, pigmentation (generalised but most common in light-exposed areas, areas exposed to pressure, mucosae, scars and palmar creases), dizziness and postural hypotension. Other recognised features include gastrointestinal symptoms (vomiting, abdominal pain and diarrhoea), arthralgia and myalgia, symptomatic hypoglycaemia, reduced axillary and pubic hair, decreased libido and, rarely, pyrexia of unknown origin. Investigations may show hyponatraemia, hyperkalaemia, increased urea, anaemia (normochromic normocytic), increased ESR, eosinophilia and mild hypercalcaemia. Causes of primary adrenal insufficiency are:

1. Autoimmune: around 70% of cases in the developed world
2. Malignancy:
   - metastatic
   - lymphoma
3. Infiltration:
   - amyloid
   - haemochromatosis
4. Infection:
   - TB
   - fungal
   - opportunistic infection, eg in AIDS

5. Shock, eg Waterhouse–Friderichsen syndrome
6. Infarction, eg secondary to antiphospholipid syndrome
7. Congenital adrenal hyperplasia
8. Congenital adrenal hypoplasia
9. Adrenomyeloneuropathy
10. Adrenoleucodystrophy
11. Adrenalectomy
12. Drugs:
    *   ketoconazole and fluconazole (inhibit cortisol synthesis)
    *   phenytoin, rifampicin (increase cortisol metabolism).

92   B: Collect blood samples for cortisol and ACTH, then give hydrocortisone 100 mg immediately, followed by intravenous fluids

The scenario suggests acute adrenal insufficiency (addisonian crisis). This is a life-threatening emergency, and should be treated urgently without waiting for the results of confirmatory tests. Clinical features include: shock (tachycardia, hypotension, poor urine output, confusion and decreased conscious level), abdominal pain, unexplained fever. Addisonian crises can be precipitated by infection, surgery and other trauma, vomiting or omission of regular gluco-corticoid medication.

Blood should be taken for urgent analysis of electrolytes and glucose, cortisol and ACTH. Hydrocortisone 100 mg should be given immediately, intravenously, and continued six hourly for 24–48 hours, or until the patient can take oral therapy. Large volumes of 0.9% NaCl may be needed to reverse the volume depletion and hyponatraemia. Patients require glucose monitoring and may require intravenous dextrose. A precipitating cause should be identified and treated where appropriate. In most cases, oral therapy can be substituted within 24–48 hours. Double the normal replacement dose should be instituted initially. Maintenance treatment in Addison's disease comprises glucocorticoid replacement (eg hydrocortisone 15 mg daily in divided doses) and mineralo-corticoid replacement (eg fludrocortisone 0.1 mg daily). Cortisol requirements increase during concurrent illness or surgery.

93   E: It is associated with von Hippel–Lindau syndrome

The majority of phaeochromocytomata secrete predominantly noradrenaline (norepinephrine). Noradrenaline mediates peripheral vasoconstriction through its action on vascular α-adrenoceptors, whereas adrenaline (epinephrine) tends to cause vasodilatation through a preferential action on vascular β-receptors. Therefore, β-blockade in the presence of high noradrenaline concentrations can result in profound α-mediated vasoconstriction, which can cause a paradoxical increase in blood pressure, digital ischaemia and infarction in severe cases. Patients may present with postural hypotension, sustained or episodic hypertension, sweating, flushing or pallor, fever, headache, paraesthesia, visual disturbances, seizures, palpitations, chest pain, dyspnoea, abdominal pain and nausea. Hypotension may a presenting feature of rare dopamine-secreting variants. Measurement of 24-hour urinary catecholamines is useful in the diagnosis of phaeochromocytoma: 90% arise within the adrenal medulla; 10%

are paragangliomas, lying outside the adrenal glands in tissue derived from the neural crest. Around 10% are multiple, 10% are inherited, and approximately 10% are malignant at initial diagnosis. There are recognised associations with:

1. MEN 2A and 2B:
   - autosomal dominant
   - mutation in ret proto-oncogene (chromosome 10)
   - hyperparathyroidism
   - medullary thyroid carcinoma
     (+ marfanoid habitus and mucosal neuromas in MEN 2B)

2. von Hippel–Lindau syndrome:
   - autosomal dominant
   - mutation in *VHL* tumour suppressor gene (chromosome 3)
   - renal cell carcinoma and renal cysts
   - cerebellar haemangioblastoma
   - retinal angiomata
   - pancreatic cysts and tumours

3. Neurofibromatosis (phaeochromocytoma in 0.5–1.0%):
   - autosomal dominant
   - mutation in *NF1* gene (chromosome 17).

Complications of phaeochromocytomata are cardiovascular (heart failure, cardiomyopathy, arrhythmia, pulmonary oedema), neurological (stroke, hypertensive encephalopathy) and diabetes mellitus. Treatments include α-blockade (eg phenoxybenzamine) and subsequent β-blockade (eg propranolol). Alpha-methylparatyrosine may limit symptoms, and high-dose ^{131}I-metaiodobenzylguanidine (MIBG) can be used to treat metastatic disease. Five-year survival is 96% for benign tumours and 44% for malignant tumours.

94 A: Colonic polyps and carcinoma are recognised associations

The history is consistent with acromegaly, which is confirmed in the glucose tolerance test (failure to suppress growth hormone (GH) to < 2 mU/l after a standard 75-g oral glucose load). The test also confirms a diagnosis of diabetes mellitus (fasting glucose ≥ 7 mmol/l and 2-hour post-glucose > 11 mmol/l). Acromegaly is the clinical condition resulting from excessive GH secretion in adults. Recognised causes are: pituitary adenoma (> 99% of cases, usually a macroadenoma), excess growth hormone-releasing hormone (GHRH) secretion (hypothalamic or ectopic) and, rarely, ectopic GH secretion.

Clinical features are increased sweating, headache, fatigue, joint pain, change in ring/shoe size, and patients often exhibit a characteristic facial appearance (coarse features, oily skin, frontal bossing, enlarged nose, prognathism), deep voice, macroglossia and skeletal changes (enlargement of hands and feet, osteoarthritis, myopathy, entrapment neuropathies such as carpal tunnel syndrome, goitre and other organomegaly). Recognised complications include hypertension, insulin resistance, obstructive sleep apnoea, increased risk of colonic polyps and colonic carcinoma, bitemporal hemianopsia, hypopituitarism and renal calculi. Insulin-like growth factor-1 (IGF-1) levels are raised in acromegaly except in severe intercurrent illness, and there is a recognised association with hypercalcaemia.

Somatostatin analogues (eg octreotide) are recognised treatments, as are dopamine agonists (eg bromocriptine, cabergoline) and the GH-receptor antagonist pegvisomant. Dopaminergic drugs may be especially helpful if there is coexistent hyperprolactinaemia.

95   E: Virilisation of female fetuses is a recognised feature
CAH is caused by a number of autosomal recessive enzyme deficiencies that result in cortisol deficiency, excess pituitary ACTH secretion and adrenal gland hyperplasia. Virilisation is a commonly recognised feature in CAH. CAH is also associated with renal salt loss and addisonian crises. The 21-hydroxylase deficiency form of CAH is not associated with hypertension, unlike those due to 11β-hydroxylase and 17α-hydroxylase deficiency. 17α-hydroxylase deficiency may cause ambiguous genitalia in male fetuses. The most common cause of CAH is 21-hydroxylase deficiency (> 90% of cases), which results in both cortisol and mineralocorticoid deficiency. The build-up of precursor steroids is channelled towards excess androgen secretion, and can lead to early onset of puberty.

11β-hydroxylase deficiency (5% of CAH) is associated with:

* Virilisation
* Precocious puberty
* Salt retention – hypernatraemia and hypokalaemia
* Hypertension.

17α-hydroxylase deficiency (reduced cortisol, androgen and oestrogen, increased mineralocorticoids) is associated with:

* Hypertension
* Hypokalaemia and hypernatraemia
* Ambiguous genitalia in male fetuses.

3β-hydroxy-steroid dehydrogenase deficiency and cholesterol desmolase deficiency are very rare.

96   B: Laurence–Moon–Biedl syndrome
This is characterised by obesity, gonadotrophin deficiency, retinitis pigmentosa, polydactyly and learning difficulties. Other recognised endocrine causes of obesity are: Cushing's syndrome (truncal obesity), hypothyroidism, hypothalamic tumours (hyperphagia), Prader–Willi syndrome (rare deletional mutation of chromosome 15q characterised by mental retardation and hypogonadotrophic hypogonadism).

Marfan's syndrome is associated with tall stature, arachnodactyly, pectus carinatum or excavatum, scoliosis, high arched palate, joint laxity and pes planus, aortic root dilatation and aortic dissection, and upward lens dislocation. It is autosomal dominant, resulting from mutation of the fibrillin-1 gene on chromosome 15.

Klinefelter's syndrome is associated with tall stature, small testes, azoospermia, reduced body hair, gynaecomastia, female-pattern fat distribution, low IQ and developmental delay. It affects about 1 in 600 males and is associated with an XXY karyotype.

Turner's syndrome is associated with short stature, and affects around 1 in 2500 females. Subjects have streak ovaries, primary amenorrhoea, infertility, low oestrogen concentrations, webbed neck, low hairline, wide carrying angle, widely spaced nipples, renal abnormalities, aortic coarctation and lymphoedema. Normal secondary sexual characteristics may develop spontaneously, or may require oestrogen stimulation.

Noonan's syndrome is associated with short stature and a phenotype similar to Turner's syndrome, but there is no XO karyotype. It is an autosomal dominant inherited syndrome and occurs in both males and females.

97   B: It is characteristically associated with hyperthyroidism

De Quervain's or subacute thyroiditis is viral in origin. Symptoms include malaise, arthralgia, fever and pain over the thyroid. It may also present with symptoms of thyrotoxicosis. Characteristically, signs include exquisite tenderness and nodularity of the thyroid gland. There is usually an elevated ESR and depressed radionuclide uptake. The patient may initially be hyperthyroid though may become hypothyroid later. In mild cases, non-steroidal anti-inflammatory drugs (NSAIDs) offer symptomatic relief, and in severe cases prednisolone may be effective. Propranolol can help control symptoms. Thyroxine replacement may be required if the patient subsequently becomes hypothyroid. Treatment with carbimazole or propylthiouracil is not indicated for treatment of thyrotoxicosis in de Quervain's thyroiditis.

98   C: Maternal diabetes is associated with neonatal hypoglycaemia

Around 2–3% of pregnant women have a diagnosis of gestational diabetes made during their pregnancy. Gestational diabetes confers a 50% chance of developing type 2 diabetes in later life. Even in well-controlled diabetes, there is an increased rate of congenital malformation and late stillbirth. Sulphonylureas can cross the placenta and stimulate production of insulin by fetal β cells, leading to neonatal macrosomia and hypoglycaemia. Pre-eclampsia is approximately four times more common in diabetic mothers than in the background population. Other recognised complications of diabetes include increased rate of congenital malformation and intrauterine death, macrosomia, neonatal hypoglycaemia and jaundice, polycythaemia and maternal infection.

99   D: The findings are due to end-organ resistance to PTH

The history and investigations suggest a diagnosis of pseudohypo-parathyroidism. Insensitivity of the PTH receptor leads to hypocalcaemia in the presence of normal or high PTH levels. It can be diagnosed using the modified Ellsworth–Howard test, where PTH infusion fails to stimulate urinary cAMP excretion (the normal response is increased cAMP excretion and decreased phosphate reabsorption). cAMP excretion may be normal in type II pseudohypoparathyroidism. The Lundh test is used to assess pancreatic exocrine function.

Type I pseudohypoparathyroidism is caused by a G-protein abnormality. It is associated with Albright's hereditary osteodystrophy (AHO), a characteristic phenotype that comprises, short stature, obesity, round face, short 4th and 5th metacarpals. Patients with type I pseudohypoparathyroidism may have resistance to the action of other hormones that rely on G-protein signalling and they should therefore be assessed for thyroid and gonadal dysfunction (due to defective thyroid-stimulating hormone (TSH) or gonadotrophin action). Type II pseudohypoparathyroidism is caused by failure of the normal response of the kidney to cAMP.

A diagnosis of pseudopseudohypoparathyroidism is unlikely as hypocalcaemia is not a recognised feature. Rehydration and/or intravenous pamidronate are appropriate management of hypercalcaemia.

100   A: Fatty acid oxidation in muscle

Insulin increases glucose transport into certain cells. It is also necessary for transmembrane transport of amino acids, glycogen formation in liver and muscle, glucose conversion to triglycerides, nucleic acid synthesis and protein synthesis. It promotes potassium and phosphate entry into cells. Therefore, an acute effect often seen in the setting of intravenous insulin administration is hypokalaemia due to intracellular potassium movement.

101   B: Graves' ophthalmopathy may cause optic neuropathy

Graves' disease is an autoimmune disorder that presents with symptoms and signs of hyperthyroidism in 90% of cases, or less commonly euthyroidism or hypothyroidism. Other features are due to the autoimmune nature of the disease, including ophthalmopathy, dermopathy, pretibial myxoedema, thyroid acropachy (resembling clubbing), diffuse goitre and lymphoid hyperplasia, and these are not directly influenced by thyroid status. Graves' dermopathy and thyroid acropachy are both due to localised accumulation of glycosaminoglycans. Graves' ophthalmopathy is characterised by swelling of the extra-ocular muscles, lymphocytic infiltration, fibrosis, muscle tethering and proliferation of orbital fat and connective tissue, and can cause proptosis, exophthalmos, optic neuropathy and ophthalmoplegia. Patients with corneal ulceration, congestive ophthalmopathy or optic neuropathy should be referred urgently to an ophthalmologist. Lid lag and lid retraction are features of the hyperthyroid state or sympathetic overactivity.

102 B: In female patients oestrogen levels are typically reduced

Anorexia nervosa typically presents in young women with weight loss, amenorrhoea and behavioural changes. There is a long-term risk of severe osteoporosis associated with more than six months of amenorrhoea. Endocrine abnormalities include:

- Deficiency of GnRH, low LH and FSH
- Low oestrogen in women and testosterone in men
- Elevated circulating cortisol (usually not suppressible with dexamethasone)
- Elevated resting GH levels
- Low-normal thyroxine, low T3 and normal TSH.

In addition, it is common to find various metabolic abnormalities, such as hyponatraemia, hypokalaemia, hypocalcaemia, hypomagnesaemia, low zinc and low phosphate levels.

103 D: The patient may have multiple endocrine neoplasia (MEN) type 1 syndrome

Hypocalcaemia is a recognised feature of acute pancreatitis. However, acute pancreatitis is a recognised complication of hypercalcaemia, and the most likely diagnosis is hyperparathyroidism, which has a prevalence of around 1 in 1000. Patients may be asymptomatic, or present with polyuria, polydipsia, anorexia, vomiting, constipation, abdominal pain, confusion, lethargy and depression.

Hyperparathyroidism can be:

- Primary – increased PTH, serum and urinary calcium, reduced serum phosphate and increased alkaline phosphatase. Caused by single adenoma (85%), hyperplasia (12%), carcinoma (<1%).
- Secondary – physiological or pathological compensatory hypertrophy of the parathyroid glands in the setting of sustained hypocalcaemia (eg chronic renal failure). PTH levels high, calcium low or normal.
- Tertiary – there is development of autonomous parathyroid hyperplasia in the setting of long-standing secondary hyperparathyroidism.

Hyperparathyroidism may result in a number of complications:

1. Bone:
   - osteoporosis
   - radiographic changes – subperiosteal resorption, pepperpot skull, rugger-jersey spine, bone cysts
   - osteitis fibrosa cystica (cystic brown tumours)
2. Kidneys:
   - renal calculi
   - nephrocalcinosis
   - renal failure

3.   Joints:
   * chondrocalcinosis
   * pseudogout
   * pancreatitis.

Once the diagnosis is made, investigation is aimed at determining the presence of end-organ damage in order to determine what intervention is indicated. Abnormal parathyroid glands should be localised preoperatively by neck exploration. ^{99m}Tc-sestamibi, thallium-technetium subtraction scanning, CT and ultrasound may be helpful. Angiography with selective venous sampling can be done at specialist centres.

Trousseau's sign refers to the precipitation of tetanic spasm in the hand by sphygmomanometer-induced ischaemia in the setting of hypocalcaemia. Hypocalcaemia, not hypercalcaemia, is associated with papilloedema and a long QT interval.

Multiple endocrine neoplasia (MEN) syndromes are syndromes with multiple benign or malignant endocrine neoplasms. MEN 1 is associated with parathyroid, pituitary and pancreatic tumours. MEN 2A is associated with parathyroid tumours, phaeochromocytoma and medullary thyroid cancer. MEN 2B is additionally associated with marfanoid habitus and mucosal neuromas.

METABOLIC MEDICINE

104 C: Immediate referral to an ophthalmologist is indicated
Diabetic nephropathy is the most common cause of end-stage renal failure in the UK and is a major cause of premature death in diabetics. It is defined as albuminuria (albumin excretion rate > 300 mg/24 hours, or a 24-hour urinary protein > 0.5 g) and declining renal function in the absence of urinary tract infection, heart failure or any other renal disease. A typical biopsy finding is nodular glomerulosclerosis (Kimmelstiel–Wilson nodules). If more widespread, this is termed diffuse glomerulosclerosis.

End-stage renal failure may require renal transplantation or dialysis. Rigorous blood pressure control reduces progression to microalbuminuria, albuminuria and end-stage renal failure. Two or more agents are usually required to control blood pressure adequately. Thiazides, β-blockers, ACE inhibitors, angiotensin-II receptor blockers (ARBs) and calcium-channel blockers have all been shown to reduce cardiovascular disease in diabetics. ACEIs and ARBs have been shown to retard the progression of diabetic nephropathy in type 2 diabetes. Intensive glycaemic control is advised, and has been shown in some studies to slow progression to albuminuria. Patients with diabetic nephropathy have a high mortality (20–100 times that of age-matched diabetics without nephropathy). This is due to cardiovascular disease in 40% of cases. Target blood pressure should be < 130/80 mmHg (and some advocate even lower targets).

Proliferative retinopathy is an indication for immediate referral to an ophthalmologist. Untreated new vessels on the disc carry a 40% risk of blindness in less than two years. Other criteria for immediate referral are rubeosis iridis/neovascular glaucoma, vitreous haemorrhage, advanced retinopathy with fibrous tissue or retinal detachments. Early referral (less than six weeks) should be made for preproliferative changes, maculopathy or a fall of more than two lines on a Snellen chart.

105 D: Intravenous thyroid hormone replacement is appropriate
The scenario suggests myxoedema coma, resulting from severe hypothyroidism; in many cases hypothyroidism has not previously been diagnosed. Precipitants include infection, trauma, cold exposure, stroke and CNS depressant drugs. Clinical features include:

- Signs of hypothyroidism (sparse hair, periorbital puffiness, dry, doughy skin, prolonged relaxation phase of tendon reflexes, obesity)
- Hypothermia
- Hypoglycaemia
- Hyponatraemia (impaired water excretion)
- Bradycardia.

Treatment involves supportive measures and mechanical ventilation may be required if there is respiratory failure. Passive external re-warming should aim for a gradual rise in temperature of no more than 0.5 °C/hour. Monitor for cardiac arrhythmias, and correct hyponatraemia and hypoglycaemia. Thyroid hormone is given by intravenous administration. Hydrocortisone is only considered in cases of adrenal insufficiency. Type II respiratory failure is likely to cause respiratory acidosis. Iodine has no role in the treatment of this condition.

106   C: Hyperosmolar non-ketotic state

This diabetic emergency occurs in older patients with type 2 diabetes, in many of whom the diagnosis has not been established. Precipitants include high sugar intake, infection, myocardial infarction, and drugs (steroids, cimetidine, phenytoin, thiazide and loop diuretics). There is normally an insidious onset, with several days of preceding ill-health, and patients are usually profoundly dehydrated at presentation due to osmotic diuresis. At presentation, confusion, coma and seizures are recognised features, along with gastroparesis and vomiting, hypercoagulable state, venous thromboses and stroke. Biochemical features are:

- Hyperglycaemia (usually > 30 mmol/l)
- High serum osmolality (> 350 mosmol/kg). This can be measured or calculated using the following equation: osmolality = 2 ([Na$^+$] + [K$^+$]) + urea + glucose
- No acidosis
- Absence of ketonuria (although this is a feature if there is prolonged vomiting).

Patients should be rehydrated and their electrolytes corrected. Insulin should be administered via continuous intravenous infusion. Precipitants should be identified and treated, and prophylactic heparin given. Central venous pressure (CVP) monitoring and urinary catheterisation are helpful.

107   D: Lugol's iodine may be effective

Thyroid crisis is a rare but life-threatening exacerbation of the manifestations of thyrotoxicosis. It is associated with a significant mortality (30–50%). Thyroid crisis may occur in hyperthyroid patients who develop acute infection, undergo surgery or receive radioiodine treatment, have antithyroid drugs withdrawn, are postpartum, or who receive radiographic contrast. Clinical features suggestive of thyroid storm are altered mental status, fever, tachyarrhythmias, vomiting, jaundice and diarrhoea. Severe cases are associated with multisystem decompensation: cardiac failure, respiratory distress, congestive hepatomegaly, dehydration and prerenal failure. Investigations may reveal a raised WBC, even in the absence of infection. Alkaline phosphatase may be raised and there may be mild hypercalcaemia. T4 and T3 will be raised but may not be grossly elevated.

Thyroid storm should be managed on an ITU where close attention can be paid to cardiorespiratory status, fluid balance and cooling. Propylthiouracil or carbimazole should be administered. Lugol's (oral iodine) solution should be given six hours later, in order to inhibit thyroid hormone release. Propranolol will control tachycardia, tremor and other adrenergic manifestations. High-dose steroid therapy can block conversion of T4 to T3. Plasmapheresis and peritoneal dialysis may be effective in cases resistant to the above measures.

108 E: Wilson's disease

This patient has presented with neurological disease, and evidence of biochemical hepatitis and type 2 (proximal) renal tubular acidosis (RTA). Wilson's is an autosomal recessive disorder (the gene is located on chromosome 13). In normal subjects ingested copper is incorporated into $\alpha 2$ globulin in the liver to form caeruloplasmin, which is the principal transport protein for copper, and necessary for biliary excretion. In Wilson's disease, copper absorption is normal but intrahepatic formation of caeruloplasmin is defective. Total body and tissue copper levels rise due to failure of biliary excretion, and urinary excretion of copper is increased. It most commonly presents in the second or third decade. Wilson's disease may be diagnosed by measuring serum caeruloplasmin (low), 24-hour urinary copper (high), liver biopsy (increased copper content) and molecular genetic testing. Treatment comprises long-term copper chelation, for example with penicillamine. Liver transplantation may be required in patients with fulminant hepatic failure and end-stage liver disease. Clinical features include:

- Hepatic disease (it can cause acute hepatitis, chronic active hepatitis and cirrhosis)
- Kayser–Fleischer corneal rings (due to deposition in Descemet's membrane)
- Arthropathy
- Haemolytic anaemia
- Neurological disease (tremor, dysarthria, dyskinesias, dysphagia and dementia)
- Proximal (type 2) renal tubular acidosis (RTA).

Proximal (type 2) RTA is typically mild with a bicarbonate (HCO_3^-) in the region of 17 or 18 mmol/l. The basic defect is proximal tubular HCO_3^- wasting due to a resetting of the T_{max} (the time taken to reach maximal drug concentration or effect) of HCO_3^- reabsorption. HCO_3^- wasting does not persist, as the plasma HCO_3^- stabilises at the concentration at which the proximal tubule is able to absorb all the filtered HCO_3^-; the urine is, therefore, typically appropriately acidified. Hypokalaemia is due to increased distal delivery of $NaHCO_3$ where Na^+ is reabsorbed at the expense of K^+. There may be other tubular abnormalities, such as glycosuria, aminoaciduria, uricosuria and phosphaturia. Diagnosis may be confirmed by measuring the fractional excretion of HCO_3^-.

109   C: Type 1 (distal) renal tubular acidosis (RTA)
This patient has a hypokalaemic, hyperchloraemic, normal anion-gap acidosis. Despite the severe systemic acidosis she has not acidified her urine. She has also had two vertebral crush fractures, an unusual occurrence without prior trauma in someone so young. In the context of the history it may suggest the presence of osteoporosis. The right loin pain suggests urinary tract infection or calculus.

Type 1 RTA is typically severe (the HCO_3^- may be reduced below 10 mmol/l). The basic defect is an inability to secrete protons in the distal tubule. This results in an inappropriate inability to acidify the urine below pH 5.3. Complications include osteoporosis, nephrocalcinosis and renal calculi. Growth failure and urinary tract infections may also occur. A renal calculus alone may be present, but this answer doesn't account for the history of fractures, the serum biochemistry and urinary pH.

Type 2 (proximal) RTA typically causes a less severe acidosis (with a HCO_3^- of 14–20 mmol/l). It causes osteomalacia and rickets rather than osteoporosis (due to phosphate wasting and reduced production of 1,25-dihydroxy D3). The basic defect is proximal tubular HCO_3^- wasting due to a resetting of the T_{max} of HCO_3^- reabsorption. In the stable state HCO_3^- wasting does not persist as the plasma HCO_3^- stabilises at the concentration at which the proximal tubule is able to absorb all the filtered HCO_3^-. Therefore, the urine is typically appropriately acidified, especially in the morning. There may be other tubular abnormalities, such as glycosuria, aminoaciduria, uricosuria and phosphaturia.

110   C: Prolonged diarrhoea
This question highlights the importance of the anion-gap: = $Na^+ + K^+ - (Cl^- + HCO_3^-)$. The normal anion gap is 12–16 mmol/l and represents unmeasured anions present on fixed or organic acids, for example albumin, phosphate, sulphate, lactate and ketones. In high anion-gap acidosis, the decreased HCO_3^- (due to buffering/titration of H^+) reflects the accumulation of unmeasured acid anions such as lactic acidosis, ketoacidosis, renal failure, drugs/toxins (salicylates, biguanides, ethylene glycol, methanol). Normal anion-gap acidosis occurs where there is loss of HCO_3^- or ingestion of H^+, and Cl^- is retained. Causes of acidosis associated with a normal anion-gap are renal tubular acidosis types 1 and 2, drugs (acetazolamide), Addison's disease, pancreatic or biliary fistulae, severe diarrhoea, ureteric diversion, ammonium chloride ingestion.

111   A: Alkaptonuria (ochronosis)
This is a rare metabolic disease inherited in an autosomal recessive manner. Homogentisic acid accumulates as a result of a deficiency in the enzyme homogentisic acid oxidase. The homogentisic acid polymerises to produce the black-brown alkapton, which is deposited in cartilage and connective tissue. Urine becomes dark on standing due to oxidation and polymerisation of homogentisic acid. Abnormal pigmentation is found in the pinna, sclerae and articular cartilage. Premature arthritis predominantly affecting the spine, and later the large joints, is a recognised feature. Intervertebral disc calcification is characteristic of alkaptonuria. The knees are commonly affected, with relative sparing of the

sacroiliac joints. The diagnosis is confirmed by measuring urinary homogentisic acid levels. Homogentisic acid is a reducing agent that gives a false-positive reaction to glucostix (as can fructose, pentose, salicylates and ascorbate).

Haemochromatosis can cause increased skin pigmentation that tends to lead to a bronze or slate-grey appearance. Patients are at increased risk of developing chondrocalcinosis or pseudogout, where calcium pyrophosphate dihydrate crystals are deposited in joint cartilage. This pyrophosphate deposition may be asymptomatic, or may cause acute attacks of pseudogout. Acute attacks most commonly affect the knee, but can affect other joints, usually large ones and mainly one at a time. X-rays may show linear calcification between and parallel to the articular surfaces. Aspiration of synovial fluid and identification of crystals by polarised light microscopy is diagnostic. Calcium pyrophosphate crystals are positively birefringent in polarising light.

Reiter's disease is a spondyloarthropathy. It is a reactive arthritis and is characterised by a triad of seronegative arthritis, conjunctivitis and urethritis. It may follow urethritis or dysentery and may be chronic or relapsing. It characteristically causes axial and/or asymmetrical large-joint oligo- or monoarthritis. It does not cause altered skin pigmentation.

112 C: Conn's syndrome
This patient has a metabolic alkalosis. Causes are:

1. Acid loss:
    - from the gastrointestinal tract (vomiting, nasogastric aspiration, antacids (in renal failure))
    - renal (diuretics, mineralocorticoids (Conn's, Cushing's), chronic hypercapnia, Bartter's syndrome, hypercalcaemia)
    - cellular (hypokalaemia)

2. Bicarbonate addition: blood transfusions (citrate), $NaHCO_3$ treatment, Milk-alkali syndrome

3. Contraction (loss of Chloride-rich/bicarbonate-poor fluid): diuretics, diarrhoea and vomiting.

Renal failure is characteristically associated with metabolic acidosis. Anxiety may be associated with hyperventilation and respiratory alkalosis. Addison's disease may be associated with a mild metabolic acidosis. Salicylate poisoning causes an early respiratory alkalosis and later metabolic acidosis.

113 C: Failure of tubular ammonium (NH_4^+) excretion
Type 4 renal tubular acidosis occurs with primary hypoaldosteronism, aldosterone resistance or, most commonly, hyporeninaemic hypoaldosteronism secondary to tubulo-interstitial disease. It is more common in elderly diabetics. The basic defect is failure of tubular NH_4^+ excretion. Type 4 RTA is characterised by a mild acidosis (HCO_3^- > 15 mmol/l), normally acidified urine and a hyperkalaemia. NSAIDs and β-blockers are recognised causes.

114   D: Ethanol toxicity

This patient has a high anion-gap acidosis. She also has a raised osmolar gap, signified by the difference between the laboratory measurement of osmolality and the estimated or expected value based on $2 \times ([Na^+] + [K^+]) + [urea] + [glucose]$. The osmolar gap is usually < 10. If it is > 10, consider methanol, ethanol, ethylene glycol, isopranolol, diethylene glycol, or, less commonly, severe hyperglycaemia and renal failure (retention of various organic and inorganic molecules).

Type 2 RTA and Addison's disease are associated with normal anion-gap acidosis. Salicylate toxicity gives a high anion-gap acidosis but doesn't produce a high osmolal gap. Conn's syndrome causes a metabolic alkalosis.

115   C: Porphyria cutanea tarda

The porphyrias are a group of inherited disorders that result from deficiency of one of the enzymes in the haem synthetic pathway. Porphyria cutanea tarda (PCT) is the commonest form of porphyria, and most commonly occurs in the setting of hepatic impairment (usually due to alcohol). Clinical features include photosensitivity, blisters, scarring, hyperpigmentation and hypertrichosis. It is caused by reduced uroporphyrinogen decarboxylase activity, and uroporphyrinogen accumulates in blood and urine during acute attacks. Excess porphyrin can be detected in the faeces between acute episodes.

116   C: Pituitary insufficiency

A key abnormality in this scenario is fasting hypoglycaemia, which can be caused by:

- Administration of insulin/sulphonylureas
- Insulinoma
- Alcohol (alcohol metabolism occurs at the expense of hepatic gluconeogenesis)
- Addison's disease
- Pituitary insufficiency (due to impaired GH and ACTH secretion)
- Liver failure
- Non-pancreatic tumours, especially retroperitoneal sarcomas
- Autoimmune hypoglycaemia, eg in Hodgkin's disease.

Polycystic ovarian syndrome is associated with insulin resistance and these patients are more likely to develop diabetes mellitus or impaired glucose tolerance. In haemochromatosis, iron may accumulate in the pancreas, leading to insulin deficiency and secondary diabetes. Corticosteroid therapy causes insulin resistance and thereby diabetes and impaired glucose tolerance. Metformin is thought to increase sensitivity to circulating insulin, which should be suppressed during fasting; metformin is not thought to cause fasting hypoglycaemia. Post-prandial hypoglycaemia can occur post-gastrectomy.

117   A: Acute intermittent porphyria

Acute intermittent porphyria (AIP) is a hereditary disorder resulting from deficiency of enzymes involved in haem synthesis. In AIP there is reduced porphobilinogen deaminase activity, and there is autosomal dominant inheritance. Females are affected more than males. Clinical features include abdominal pain, vomiting and constipation, peripheral neuropathy (mainly motor), hypertension, tachycardia, autonomic neuropathy, convulsions and psychiatric disturbance. Findings during acute episodes include fever, papilloedema, raised WBC and ESR, hyponatraemia, and features of syndrome of inappropriate ADH secretion (SIADH). Unlike other forms of porphyria, AIP is not associated with photosensitivity or rash. Precipitants include stress, infection and drugs (alcohol, benzodiazepines, rifampicin, oral contraceptives, phenytoin and sulphonamides).

Investigations show elevated δ-aminolaevulinic acid (δALA) and porphobilinogen (PBG) levels in urine and serum, and red cell PBG deaminase is reduced and δALA synthetase is increased. Treatment comprises avoidance of precipitants, high carbohydrate intake, haem arginine and supportive management.

NEPHROLOGY

118   A: Focal and segmental glomerulonephritis
The history and raised ANA titres suggest a connective tissue disorder, which has manifest as distal small-joint and skin involvement. The facial rash might be distributed in a wolverine pattern, suggesting systemic lupus erythematosus (SLE). This diagnosis is supported by the elevated ESR but comparatively normal CRP level. Hypertension is a common feature in chronic renal impairment, regardless of the underlying aetiology, and may be particularly important in SLE. While renal changes of hypertension may be identified, these are not expected to be predominant in the histological picture. The cardinal pathological diagnostic features involve glomerular abnormalities, which have been classified on the basis of morphology by the World Health Organisation: class 1 – normal morphology, class 2 – mesangioproliferative glomerulo-nephropathy (GN), class 3 – focal and segmental proliferative GN, class 4 – diffuse proliferative GN, class 5 – membranous GN. Kimmelstiel–Wilson lesions are pathognomonic of diabetic nephropathy, and represent glomerulosclerosis. Renal cholesterol embolisation is often preceded by vascular access procedures. Cases of spontaneous embolisation are associated with impaired renal function and a raised ESR is a recognised feature. However, rash rarely involves the face and appears to be a vasculitic rash affecting the peripheries.

119   E: Ureteric calculi
Adult polycystic kidney disease (APKD) is a genetic condition due to autosomal dominant inheritance of abnormalities of the *PKD1* gene (chromosome 16) or *PKD2* gene (chromosome 4). Genetic counselling is important. Characteristic features include irregular, enlarged kidneys with multiple cysts of varying size. Clinical features include recurrent urinary tract infections, calculi, hypertension and impaired renal function. In APKD, there are a number of recognised associations, including intracranial aneurysms, subarachnoid haemorrhage, mitral valve prolapse, and multiple cysts within the liver (40%) and pancreas (25%). Clinical review is important for monitoring blood pressure and renal function, with preparation for haemodialysis or transplantation if appropriate.

120   B: Nephrotic syndrome

Nephrotic syndrome is characterised by heavy urinary protein loss, due to glomerulopathy which causes hypoalbuminaemia, hypercholesterolaemia and renal impairment. Increased risk of deep venous thrombosis is a recognised feature of nephrotic syndrome, and is likely to account for the presenting leg symptoms. The histological diagnoses most often identified in nephrotic syndromes are minimal-change glomerulonephritis (30%), membranous glomerulonephropathy (25%), focal segmental glomerulonephritis (15%) and mesangiocapillary glomerulonephritis (10%). In around 5–10% of cases with membranous GN appearance, an underlying malignancy is present, which is usually identified at the time of diagnosis. Many patients respond to high-dose corticosteroids, and immunosuppressive treatment in certain cases.

121   E: Wegener's granulomatosis

Wegener's granulomatosis is a necrotising arteritis that most commonly involves the kidney, upper airways and lungs. It characteristically presents as glomerulonephritis in association with epistaxis, haemoptysis, rhinitis, sinusitis, otitis media, oral ulceration and abnormal chest X-ray. Typical chest X-ray appearances include diffuse, patchy opacification (resembling pulmonary oedema) and isolated or multiple lung nodules. Diagnosis is confirmed by the presence of cANCA, which can be used for disease monitoring. It is a potentially fatal condition. Treatment includes high-dose corticosteroids and pulsed cyclophosphamide treatment. Mesangial IgA disease (IgA nephropathy) commonly presents in young males as haematuria during intercurrent illness, but respiratory complications are not a recognised feature. Rhabdomyolysis may be associated with renal impairment, metabolic acidosis, hypocalcaemia, hyperkalaemia and a raised creatinine phosphokinase concentration, but would not account for the upper or lower respiratory tract complications in this scenario. Goodpasture's syndrome (anti-glomerular basement membrane disease) often presents with features of glomerulonephritis and haemoptysis. However, upper respiratory complications and raised cANCA are not recognised features, which makes this a less likely diagnosis.

122   E: Ureteric obstruction

The scenario presents a patient recently commenced on warfarin who has a life-threatening INR. The flank bruising is strongly suggestive of retroperitoneal bleeding, presumably as a haemorrhagic consequence of the poorly controlled INR level. While a low haemoglobin concentration might suggest chronic renal impairment, it is also consistent with blood loss in the setting of acute renal impairment. Ureteric obstruction and obstructive nephropathy are recognised complications of retroperitoneal bleeding due to excess warfarin treatment. Assuming that the premorbid renal function was normal, autoregulatory mechanisms would be expected to maintain renal function in the setting of mild to moderate hypovolaemia. Recurrent renal thromboembolism might explain a stepwise chronic deterioration in renal function but is more likely to occur in the absence of anticoagulation, and particularly unlikely where the INR is so high. Acute pancreatitis is made unlikely by the normal WBC; normal serum amylase values are < 100 U/l but these increase in the presence of renal impairment. Typically, in the setting of acute pancreatitis, a diagnostic value for amylase would be > 1000 U/l.

123 D: Urinary osmolality of 205 mosmol/kg

Prerenal uraemia is usually a consequence of impaired renal blood flow, and may be a consequence of shock, haemorrhage or intravascular fluid volume depletion. A lesser haemodynamic compromise is sufficient to provoke pre-renal uraemia in patients with existing renal artery insufficiency, most commonly due to diffuse atherosclerosis. It is often accompanied by activation of the renin-angiotensin-aldosterone axis as a compensatory mechanism, which causes sodium retention (hence low urinary sodium < 10 mmol/l) and production of small amounts of concentrated urine (> 350 mosmol/kg). Clinical signs associated with intravascular volume depletion include low JVP, low systemic blood pressure, reduced skin turgor, dry mouth and cool peripheries; raised JVP does not exclude significant volume depletion, as there may be an alternative cause, for example coexistent right heart failure. In acute tubular necrosis, there is a hallmark inability to retain sodium so that urinary sodium remains normal. Red cell casts do not strongly suggest either diagnosis, and are more typically found in glomerulonephritis. Tubular cell casts may be found in acute tubular necrosis.

124 C: Hyperuricaemia

The risks of contrast nephropathy are dose-dependent. Other factors associated with substantially increased risk are dehydration, loop diuretic treatment, hyponatraemia, and pre-existing renal impairment, diabetes mellitus and advanced age. Theophylline appears to reduce the risk of contrast nephropathy, possibly by inhibiting the vascular effects of adenosine, although this has not been confirmed in large randomised controlled studies. Patients with asthma are at increased risk of acute attacks, bronchospasm and anaphylactoid reactions, although there is no apparent increase in the risk of contrast nephropathy.

125 D: Salicylate

The effectiveness of haemodialysis will be determined by the volume of distribution of drug, protein binding, and its physicochemical properties. Amiodarone has an extremely wide volume of distribution, such that comparatively small amounts of the total body amount are found in the circulation and haemodialysis is ineffective. Digoxin is cleared fairly rapidly by renal elimination and, in cases of severe toxicity, digoxin-specific antibody (Digibind®) is an effective means of enhancing drug clearance. Paracetamol, even after large overdoses, is cleared comparatively rapidly by hepatic metabolism; the clinical consequences (particularly liver damage) often lag behind and manifest when paracetamol has already been cleared. Salicylates, lithium, ethylene glycol, alcohol, methanol and theophylline are effectively cleared by dialysis. Rebound effects may occur as drug redistributes from tissues to blood (especially with lithium), and repeated or continuous dialysis may be required.

126   A: Bilateral small kidneys on ultrasound scan
This is strongly suggestive of chronic, rather than acute, renal failure. It should be remembered that kidney size may remain normal in chronic renal failure (CRF), or kidneys may be enlarged (adult polycystic kidney disease, amyloidosis, infiltrative disorders). Hypertension, hyperkalaemia and proteinuria are common features of both chronic and acute renal impairment. Normocytic anaemia, in the absence of other causes, is suggestive of chronic renal impairment, though this is also a recognised feature of acute renal failure due to haemolytic uraemic syndrome or systemic vasculitis.

127   C: Renal scarring virtually never occurs beyond 8 years of age
Ureteric re-implantation is rarely performed now as a result of better screening, and early institution of prophylactic antibiotics. It is recognised that offspring have around a 20% chance of inheriting reflux nephropathy. Chronic pyelonephritis is now an uncommon cause of renal failure, and only a very small proportion of patients develop progressive chronic renal failure. Evidence of urinary infection is found in only around half of all patients. Reflux nephropathy has a higher prevalence among patients with abnormal renal anatomy, but the majority of patients with reflux nephropathy have 'normal' anatomy.

128   B: Chronic renal impairment
The anaemia is associated with a normal MCV, suggesting a normocytic type, which is consistent with that seen in chronic renal impairment. An alternative is a mixed deficiency of iron and vitamin B_{12} or folate, and in this case the blood film revealed mixed populations of microcytic and macrocytic red cells such that the MCV was normal. An additional measure provided by many laboratories is the red cell distribution width, which reports variability in red cell size (normally 11.5–14.5%) and can help distinguish between a normocytic population and a mixed red cell population (red cell distribution width would be increased in the latter). In the present scenario, a mixed haematinic deficiency is unlikely because folate and B_{12} deficiency are typically associated with a megaloblastic anaemia (MCV usually > 110 fl), and reduced WBC and platelet counts. Antiphospholipid antibody syndrome is often associated with a microcytic hypochromic anaemia and thrombocytopenia due to autoantibody binding to erythrocyte and platelet populations respectively. Coeliac disease is typically associated with a hypochromic microcytic anaemia, due to iron malabsorption. Hypothyroidism is a recognised cause of a simple macrocytosis.

Serum creatinine concentration is a poor marker of renal function and is additionally influenced by lean muscle mass, age, sex and race. In particular, serum concentrations may appear surprisingly normal in the presence of severe renal failure in the setting of substantially reduced muscle bulk or previous limb amputation. It is important to consider serial measurement to detect deterioration in renal function, and creatinine clearance can be estimated using the Cockcroft–Gault equation. A 24-hour urinary collection may help, but in practice is often incomplete. The current gold standard measure of glomerular filtration is measurement of isotope (EDTA or DTPA) excretion.

129 B: She is likely to have mutation of the *PKD1* gene, encoding polycystin 1

The finding of proteinuria and the abnormal ultrasound scan findings are strongly suggestive of adult polycystic kidney disease (APKD). Multiple renal cysts, which may or may not contain a visible fluid level, are a pathognomonic feature. Extrarenal cysts are commonly found, typically involving the liver and pancreas. There is a mutation of the *PKD1* gene in around 85% of patients, and of the *PKD2* gene in around 10% of patients, and the disorder is transmitted in an autosomal dominant manner. The lack of family history should not dissuade you from making the diagnosis, and relevant family members should be screened. In the majority of patients, there is a gradual decline in renal function, progressing to dialysis dependence but the rate of decline is highly variable. Deterioration of renal function is delayed by good blood pressure control and prompt treatment of any complications that might arise, such as infection, ureteric calculi and anaemia. In this patient, the risks to the fetus and mother are comparatively small, given the apparently normal blood pressure and renal function but close monitoring will be required throughout the pregnancy. Fetal and neonatal ultrasonography will be ineffective because renal cysts typically do not become apparent until adolescence, and ultrasound screening is typically reserved until at least 18 years of age.

130 B: Nephrotic syndrome associated with minimal-change nephropathy

The diagnosis of nephrotic syndrome is strongly suggested by the clinical features of facial and peripheral oedema, along with heavy proteinuria, hypoalbuminaemia and impaired renal function. Proteinuria should be formally quantified, and is typically greater than 2 g per day. Nephritis tends to present with mixed proteinuria and haematuria, but proteinuria is less prominent and hypoalbuminaemia is unusual. Pyelonephritis might account for haematuria and proteinuria, but would not explain the other clinical and investigation findings. SIADH causes hyponatraemia, but proteinuria and hypoalbuminaemia are not recognised features. Renal amyloidosis is often associated with microalbuminuria and, uncommonly, can be associated with a more severe protein-losing nephropathy. In nephrotic syndrome, renal biopsy is important because the pathological features can determine prognosis and most appropriate treatment. Minimal-change nephropathy is the commonest pathological form, identified in around a quarter of all cases, and is associated with the greatest chance of remission. Other recognised associations in nephrotic syndrome include hypercholesterolaemia and increased risk of thrombosis and vascular occlusion. Significant haematuria is unusual in uncomplicated nephrotic syndrome, and suggests the possibility of renal vein thrombosis.

131 A: ANCA-associated vasculitis
The most likely underlying cause in this situation is ANCA-associated vasculitis. Haemoptysis and diffuse opacification on plain chest X-ray can be caused by pulmonary haemorrhage, pulmonary oedema or infection. Measurement of CO transfer and high-resolution chest CT scanning may be required to distinguish these, and bronchoscopy and bronchoalveolar lavage may be required in some cases. The initial treatment of all ANCA-associated vasculitides is similar, although the distinction between pANCA and cANCA is important as a determinant of future relapse rate, extrarenal vasculitic manifestations and overall prognosis. Less likely diagnoses include mixed essential cryo-globulinaemia (underlying hepatitis C in 50% of these cases), systemic lupus erythematosus and Henoch–Schönlein purpura. The clinical features of toxic shock syndrome arise from the effects of a toxin (TSST-1) liberated most commonly in the setting of *Staphylococcus aureus* infection but this would rarely present with a progressive history over one week, and the clinical features are typically overshadowed by shock, poor tissue perfusion and hypotension.

132 B: Osteomalacia
In proximal (type 2) renal tubular acidosis, the principal metabolic defects arise due to a failure of proximal tubules to reabsorb phosphate, amino acids, glucose and uric acid (Fanconi's syndrome). This is in contrast to distal (type 1) renal tubular acidosis, in which there is failure of the distal tubules to actively secrete hydrogen ions. Due to phosphate wasting in type 2 renal tubular acidosis, there is often secondary hyperparathyroidism and osteomalacia is a well-recognised complication. Type 2 renal tubular acidosis is usually secondary to Wilson's disease (in which hypouricaemia is a characteristic feature) and myeloma; it is rarely the primary idiopathic disorder. Metabolic acidosis is generally less severe than in type 1 renal tubular acidosis, because in the setting of acidosis, less bicarbonate becomes available for glomerular filtration and loss in the urine. Nephrocalcinosis and renal calculi are not recognised features, though they are characteristic features of type 1 renal tubular acidosis.

133 C: Prednisolone
A number of mechanical causes may account for acute renal failure post-transplantation, even if there are no immediate operative complications, including transplant renal vein thrombosis, renal artery occlusion and ureteric obstruction. Urinary sepsis is a recognised cause of acute deterioration in the graft kidney. ACE inhibitors may precipitate acute renal impairment, particularly if the arterial anastomoses are poor. Ciclosporin is commonly used for immunosuppression post-renal transplant, and is a recognised cause of direct nephrotoxicity and hyperkalaemia. It is cleared predominantly by renal excretion and therefore blood levels can increase, causing further toxicity. There is a good relationship between plasma concentration and likely nephrotoxicity and therapeutic drug monitoring is indicated. Acute graft rejection is an important cause of early renal failure, and renal biopsy may be required to establish the diagnosis.

GASTROENTEROLOGY

134 B: Antimitochondrial antibodies and liver biopsy
Options A, B, C and D are all useful in confirming the diagnosis, but B would be the most sensitive and specific means of confirming the diagnosis. Antimitochondrial antibodies are positive in more than 95% of patients. Liver biopsy will show characteristic features of destruction of the intralobular ducts, small-duct proliferation, fibrosis and cirrhosis. pANCA and liver biopsy are the most reliable tests for confirming a diagnosis of autoimmune hepatitis.

135 D: Primary biliary cirrhosis
Primary biliary cirrhosis (PBC) characteristically occurs in middle-aged women (90% of patients are female). Destruction of small intrahepatic ducts by chronic inflammation leads to progressive cholestasis, cirrhosis and portal hypertension. PBC may be asymptomatic. Other clinical features are pruritus, cholestatic jaundice, skin pigmentation, xanthelasmata secondary to hyper-cholesterolaemia, clubbing and hepatosplenomegaly. PBC may be complicated by osteoporosis. Malabsorption of fat-soluble vitamins results in osteomalacia and coagulopathy. Other complications include portal hypertension, ascites, variceal haemorrhage, hepatic encephalopathy and hepatocellular carcinoma. The cause unknown, although it appears to be autoimmune and is strongly associated with other autoimmune diseases.

Blood tests reveal cholestatic liver function tests (LFTs) predominantly raised alkaline phosphatase and gamma-glutamyl transpeptidase (GGT). More than 95% of patients are anti-mitochondrial antibody positive, and have raised IgM. Abdominal ultrasound and ERCP are useful to exclude extrahepatic cholestasis. Liver biopsy shows destruction of the intralobular ducts, small duct proliferation, fibrosis and cirrhosis.

Treatment includes symptomatic therapy, fat-soluble vitamin supplements and liver transplantation. Ursodeoxycholic acid may reduce time to transplantation.

Primary sclerosing cholangitis (PSC) could present with these clinical features. However, the age and gender of the patient are a clue to the answer. Furthermore, PSC is strongly associated with inflammatory bowel disease (particularly ulcerative colitis) and HIV infection, and questions about it would be more likely to mention one of these in the history. The raised cholesterol and IgM are also more in keeping with primary biliary cirrhosis than PSC.

Autoimmune hepatitis would not typically present with an obstructive jaundice: LFTs would be hepatitic; IgG would be preferentially increased (rather than IgM); and hypercholesterolaemia is not a feature.

Alcoholic cirrhosis is possible but no mention of alcohol has been made in the question. This answer doesn't really account for the hypercholesterolaemia, positive anti-smooth muscle antibody and raised IgM.

Gallstone disease can cause an obstructive jaundice (if a stone blocks the common bile duct). This would be expected to cause abdominal pain, jaundice or fever, although it can be asymptomatic. Prolonged biliary obstruction or repeated attacks can lead to secondary biliary cirrhosis but this is now rare. The positive anti-smooth muscle antibody and raised IgM are also against this answer.

136   C: Familial Mediterranean fever

Familial Mediterranean fever is an autosomal recessive disease characterised by recurrent serositis. Patients present with fever, abdominal pain, pleurisy and arthritis, with resolution between attacks. Amyloidosis is a complication and is a probable cause of malabsorption and nephrotic syndrome. Steatorrhoea suggests:

- Lack of lipase activity, eg secondary to pancreatic disease, Zollinger–Ellison syndrome
- Bile salt deficiency, eg biliary obstruction, interrupted enterohepatic circulation, bacterial overgrowth
- Decreased absorption due to resection small bowel, damage to mucosal cells or increased transit
- Impaired transport of chylomicrons.

Failure to absorb xylose and excrete it in the urine indicates small bowel mucosal disease. Normal absorption would suggest pancreatic insufficiency. False positives may occur rarely in pancreatic disease and as a result of delayed gastric emptying, poor renal function or poor gastric output. The pleural effusion may be a consequence of hypoalbuminaemia.

Jejunal or rectal biopsy would be a helpful investigation. Amyloidosis is diagnosed after Congo-red staining of affected tissue, and the risk of developing amyloidosis in Familial Mediterranean fever is reduced by prophylactic colchicine.

137   A: Eradication therapy is indicated if found in a patient with peptic ulcer disease

Helicobacter pylori is a Gram-negative spiral bacillus that exists within gastric mucosa. It is present in 70% of patients with gastric ulcer and in 90% of those with duodenal ulcer (compared with 50% of control subjects). It is associated with chronic atrophic gastritis, gastric carcinoma and gastric lymphoma, but not autoimmune gastritis. It produces ammonia via the enzyme urease, which can neutralise the local acidic pH, and this is the basis of the urease and urea breath tests. Other methods of detection include antral biopsy at endoscopy, with haematoxylin and eosin or Giemsa staining, culture and *H. pylori* serology (although this remains positive despite treatment). *H. pylori* stimulates gastrin release, which leads to increased parietal cell mass and increased acid output (and may be responsible for the production of gastric metaplasia and duodenal ulcers).

All patients with peptic ulcer disease should be considered for at least one attempt at eradication. Eradication regimes vary, but most involve a proton pump inhibitor and at least two antibiotics because antibiotic resistance develops quickly.

Hydrogen breath tests may be used to detect carbohydrate malabsorption, small bowel bacterial overgrowth and mouth-to-caecal transit time.

138 D: Patients commonly present with diarrhoea and steatorrhoea

Zollinger–Ellison syndrome is a rare condition with a prevalence of one per million. Gastrin-secreting adenomas cause severe gastric and duodenal ulceration. Ulcers may also occur elsewhere in the small intestine. The tumour is usually pancreatic in origin, although may occur in the stomach, duodenum or spleen. Around 50–60% are malignant, 10% are at multiple sites and 30% are associated with MEN 1. Clinical features include pain and dyspepsia (from multiple ulcers) and malabsorption, steatorrhoea and diarrhoea. The latter symptoms arise because of acid-related inactivation of digestive enzymes and damage to small bowel mucosa.

Diagnosis is suggested by very high fasting serum gastrin levels and elevated basal gastric acid output. There is a rise in gastrin secretion with secretin (unlike the high gastrin seen in achlorhydria). CT scanning may help locate the tumour and assess for metastases. Treatment comprises acid suppression with high doses of proton pump inhibitor drugs, surgical resection of adenoma, and somatostatin analogues to reduce diarrhoea and gastrin secretion.

Necrolytic migratory erythema is a recognised feature in over 90% of patients with glucagonoma.

139 C: Jejunal biopsy is likely to show villous atrophy

The investigations show a mixed anaemia (iron deficiency plus folate or vitamin B_{12} deficiency), and features of hyposplenisim. This strongly suggests an underlying diagnosis of coeliac disease. The underlying condition involves gluten-sensitive enteropathy, and patients are intolerant of wheat, barley, rye and oats. It affects 0.1–0.2% of the population, and onset may be at any age. There is villous atrophy on jejunal biopsy, which reverses on a gluten-free diet. Clinical features include: diarrhoea, abdominal discomfort, aphthous oral ulceration, weight loss, anaemia (usually iron deficiency, but folate and B_{12} if severe), increased incidence of small bowel lymphoma, hyposplenism (Howell–Jolly bodies on the blood film), osteomalacia due to vitamin D malabsorption, and features secondary to malabsorption of other fat-soluble vitamins (A, E and K). Recognised features are dermatitis herpetiformis (an itchy vesicular rash affecting extensor surfaces), IgA deficiency (2% of coeliacs, 15 times the prevalence in the general population) and organ-specific autoimmune disease.

Factors aiding diagnosis are: antiendomysial and antigliadin antibodies (false negatives in Ig A deficiency) and jejunal biopsy. Treatment is with a gluten-free diet, and supplementation of haematinics and vitamins if required.

140   D: May cause myoclonic epilepsy
Whipple's disease is a rare multisystem condition, occurring predominantly in middle-aged white men. The organism responsible is *Tropheryma whippelii* (a Gram-positive actinomycete). Although primarily a small bowel disorder, other clinical features are:

* Diarrhoea and malabsorption secondary to villous atrophy
* Seronegative non-deforming arthropathy
* Pyrexia of unknown origin
* Splenomegaly
* Endocarditis
* Dementia
* Supranuclear ophthalmoplegia
* Myoclonic epilepsy.

Diagnosis is by jejunal biopsy, which shows macrophages containing periodic acid-Schiff- (PAS) positive granules within villi, and there may be villous atrophy. Treatment requires continuous antibiotics for at least a year.

141   E: Porphyria cutanea tarda
Porphyria cutanea tarda tends to present in patients with chronic liver disease, particularly alcoholic liver disease. It is characterised by rash and photosensitivity and, in contrast to acute intermittent porphyria, severe abdominal pain is not a recognised feature. Abdominal pain is a feature of each of the other potential stems. Henoch–Schönlein purpura is a recognised cause of intestinal intussusception, and familial Mediterranean fever can be associated with recurrent episodes of polyserositis.

142   E: Patients may present with exertional wheeze
Carcinoid syndrome occurs when vasoactive mediators produced by carcinoid tumours reach the systemic circulation. Carcinoid tumours arise from neuroendocrine cells and produce a variety of hormones and vasoactive substances, most commonly serotonin. Other products include adreno-corticotrophic hormone (ACTH), growth hormone-releasing hormone (GHRH), parathyroid hormone (PTH), histamine, substance P, prostaglandins, kallikrein and dopamine. Gastrointestinal tumours do not give rise to the syndrome in the absence of liver metastases.

Clinical features of carcinoid syndrome include:
* Flushing
* Diarrhoea
* Bronchospasm
* Pellagra – nicotinic acid deficiency may occur secondary to excessive tryptophan metabolism
* Arthritis
* Sclerotic bone metastases
* Carcinoid heart disease – thickening and retraction of the heart valves (particularly the tricuspid and pulmonary valves) may occur, leading to valvular stenosis and regurgitation.

It may be diagnosed by urinary 5-HIAA assay. Abdominal ultrasound, CT and MRI can localise the tumour and detect metastatic spread. Radionuclide scanning with radiolabelled octreotide can help locate metastatic disease. Radiolabelled ^{123}I-MIBG and PET scanning can also be used to identify carcinoid tumour.

Treatment options for carcinoid syndrome include surgery, somatostatin analogues (eg octreotide), hepatic embolisation, radiotherapy (for palliation of bone or CNS metastases), chemotherapy, radiolabelled isotope therapy (octreotide or MIBG), and interferon-α. The prognosis is variable. The five-year survival rate with liver metastases is about 20–40%, with a median survival time of two years.

143 C: No specific treatment is required

The investigations are strongly suggestive of Gilbert's syndrome, which is a congenital hyperbilirubinaemia inherited in an autosomal dominant fashion, and present in 2–5% of the population. It is caused by reduced conjugating enzymes. There appears to be impaired bilirubin uptake by hepatocytes, which leads to a rise in unconjugated bilirubin concentrations. Unconjugated bilirubin is water insoluble, and so it does not appear in the urine. Fasting, stress, intercurrent illness and intravenous nicotinic acid produce a rise in plasma bilirubin. Gilbert's syndrome is asymptomatic. It may present with jaundice or be detected during routine testing.

144 C: Mixed essential cryoglobulinaemia

The others conditions listed are recognised associations with hepatitis B. In hepatitis C, a serum sickness-type illness often occurs. Immune complex deposition can lead to membranous or membranoproliferative glomerulo-nephritis. Polyarteritis nodosa and other vasculitides tend to occur in chronic infection, but may also be a feature of acute illness. Neurological abnormalities may be secondary to vasculitis or Guillain–Barré syndrome. Haematological abnormalities may occur, the most dangerous being aplastic anaemia.

145 B: Blood levels of HBeAg correlate with infectivity

HBeAg and HBV DNA correlate with viral replication, and hence infectivity. The virus may be found in cell types other than hepatocytes, for example renal tubules, lymph nodes. This may partly explain recurrence after transplantation. Around 10% develop chronic infection. IgG HBcAb alone implies continuing viral replication. IgG HBcAb in low titres, together with HBsAb, indicates a previous, cleared, infection. Patients who are immunodeficient are more likely to develop chronic viral hepatitis.

146 B: Chronic liver disease occurs in 50-80% of those infected

Hepatitis C is an RNA virus. Interferon-α results in clearance of the virus in only 25% of patients with chronic liver disease. It initially leads to normalisation of liver function and loss of hepatitis C virus RNA in 50% of patients; six months later, however, 50% of these are positive again. Ribavirin is also used to treat chronic infection. Fulminant hepatic failure is a recognised complication, but is very rare. Transmission is by sexual contact, via contaminated blood or through infected needle sharing among intravenous drug users.

147 B: Autoimmune hepatitis

Autoimmune hepatitis is characterised by the production of autoantibodies directed against hepatocytes. It may present with an acute hepatitis or with chronic illness. Clinical features include lethargy, abdominal discomfort, arthralgia, myalgia and jaundice. It is commoner in females (female to male ratio 4:1), and two main types are recognised, according to the presence of circulating autoantibodies:

Type I: antinuclear antibodies (ANA) and/or anti-smooth muscle antibodies (SMA)
Type II: anti-liver kidney microsomal (LKM) antibodies.

It is associated with:
- Autoimmune thyroid disease
- Autoimmune haemolytic anaemia
- Pernicious anaemia
- Ulcerative colitis
- Diabetes
- Glomerulonephritis
- HLA-DR3, -DR4, -A1 and -B8.

Investigations typically show raised ALT and IgG, ANA- or SMA-positive in 80%, LKM antibody-positive in 3–4%, pANCA positive in 90%, and a mononuclear cell infiltrate of portal and periportal areas, with piecemeal necrosis, fibrosis or cirrhosis on liver biopsy.

Treatment usually comprises steroids and azathioprine. Newer drugs, such as tacrolimus, ciclosporin and mycophenolate mofetil appear to be beneficial. Liver transplantation may be indicated in chronic disease or fulminant/subfulminant hepatic failure.

148 C: Metronidazole and diloxanide are effective treatments

Amoebic liver abscesses are caused by infection with *Entamoeba histolytica*. Patients typically present with fever and right upper-quadrant pain, and 5–10% have bloody diarrhoea. Abscesses are usually single, and can be diagnosed by ultrasound scan or CT, supported by serological testing. Drainage of the cysts yields anchovy-like pus. Amoebic abscesses are treated with metronidazole and diloxanide to eradicate luminal organisms. Hydatid liver cysts are caused by ingestion of *Echinococcus granulosus* eggs (from dogs and cattle). Eggs hatch in the intestine and migrate to the liver. Calcified, septate cysts occur in the liver. Patients present with fever, hepatomegaly and eosinophilia. Rupture of cysts may cause anaphylactoid-type reactions.

Hydatid cysts, not amoebic abscesses, are commonly calcified and loculated. There is usually a long latent period between the diarrhoeal illness and the development of a liver abscess and the stools are therefore often clear. The Casoni skin test is an immediate hypersensitivity test used to detect sensitisation to hydatid antigen. It may be used to diagnose hydatid disease. In amoebic liver disease serology is positive in more than 90%.

149 A: Hepatic encephalopathy

Hyponatraemia can be 'true' in association with Addison's disease and diuretic use, or be dilutional in cases of fluid overload, for example in congestive heart failure, renal failure or hepatic failure. Renal impairment is typically associated with hyperkalaemia and excluded by the normal creatinine concentration. A low urea concentration is consistent with impaired hepatic synthetic function. Gastroenteritis and sepsis would typically be associated with a raised urea concentration. Metformin is associated with lactic acidosis, particularly in the presence of renal impairment. Brisk reflexes and plantar responses suggest encephalopathy. Viral encephalitis is typically associated with a raised CSF protein concentration. Further investigations include INR, iron studies (haemochromatosis may be the underlying cause), liver biochemistry, EEG and liver biopsy. Alcoholic liver disease is the most likely underlying cause.

150 D: Irritable bowel syndrome

Irritable bowel syndrome (IBS) is characterised by more than three months of at least two of the following: abdominal pain related to defecation, constipation or diarrhoea, and subjective change in the quantity or quality of stool. It is very common and affects as many as 20% of patients referred to hospital with abdominal symptoms. The aetiology is thought to be related to abnormal gastrointestinal autonomic function, such that gastrointestinal motility is erratic and sensitivity to luminal pressure is increased. Around 70–80% of cases affect women, and there is a strong association with depressive illness. Inflammatory bowel disease is made unlikely by the normal appearance of the rectal mucosa. Colonic carcinoma and familial polyposis coli (FPC) are typically asymptomatic in the early stages, and may present due to occult gastrointestinal blood loss.

HAEMATOLOGY

151   C: Renal carcinoma
The haematological indices indicate polycythaemia. Stress polycythaemia is unlikely because renal function is normal; usually urea is increased in keeping with reduced plasma volume. Polycythaemia rubra vera is typically associated with elevated WBC and or platelet count. Secondary polycythaemia can be secondary to chronic hypoxia (eg regular smoking, chronic lung disease, cyanotic heart disease or sleep apnoea), which is made unlikely by the normal arterial blood gas results. Alternatively, polycythaemia can be associated with underlying malignancy, for example hepatoma, renal tumours, cerebellar haemangiomata, or uterine carcinoma.

152   D: Disseminated intravascular coagulation
Disseminated intravascular coagulation (DIC) is a recognised complication of surgery, sepsis or underlying malignancy. Pathognomonic features include thrombocytopenia due to consumption of platelets in peripheral microthrombi, elevated APPT and INR due to consumption of coagulation factors, abnormal bleeding and tendency to vascular occlusion. Factors V and VIII have comparatively short half-lives, and are the most readily consumed factors. Fibrinogen degradation products (FDPs) are usually elevated, and help to establish the diagnosis. Treatment should be directed at treating the underlying cause where possible, and support by way of platelet, fresh frozen plasma and whole blood transfusion where appropriate.

153   D: Paroxysmal nocturnal haemoglobinuria
Paroxysmal nocturnal haemoglobinuria (PNH) is a disorder characterised by increased complement-mediated destruction of red blood cells, granulocytes and platelets, and most commonly presents with pancytopenia. Long-standing haemoglobinuria is often complicated by chronic renal impairment due to pyelonephritis, papillary necrosis and tubular necrosis. Iron deficiency is common due to chronic intravascular haemolysis and urinary iron loss. Patients with PNH are prone to arterial and venous occlusion, which can present as intracranial or intra-abdominal thrombosis. A rare but recognised complication is progression to acute leukaemia or myelodysplasia.

154 B: Henoch–Schönlein purpura

Purpuric rash is typically caused by impaired platelet function or small vessel dysfunction. Henoch–Schönlein purpura is associated with microvascular dysfunction, and the platelet count and platelet function are essentially normal. The aetiology is unclear and most cases remit spontaneously within four to eight weeks. The rash is typically distributed over the lower limbs, buttocks and lower back. Associated features are colicky abdominal pain, gastrointestinal bleeding and renal impairment. There is no known effective treatment, and corticosteroids are of no value. It is most prevalent in children and young adults, and becomes less common with advancing age.

155 B: Diffuse pulmonary lymphoma

The abnormally high lymphocytosis, lymphadenopathy and hepato-splenomegaly are strongly suggestive of underlying chronic lymphocytic leukaemia. In the majority of advanced cases there is suppression of immunoglobulin production (immune paresis), and in some instances paraprotein is detected. This predisposes to recurrent chest infections in most patients. In this case the pulmonary function tests (PFTs) are consistent with a restrictive lung defect, which is most likely to represent diffuse pulmonary infiltration. A similar pattern of PFTs would be expected in pulmonary fibrosis, for example due to sarcoidosis, but these are less satisfactory explanations in the context of established chronic lymphocytic leukaemia.

156 C: Hypothyroidism

The blood picture indicates a macrocytosis, and the normal bone marrow examination indicates that it is non-megaloblastic. Typical causes include hypothyroidism, alcohol excess, liver disease and abnormal lipid metabolism. Non-megaloblastic macrocytosis is rarely associated with an MCV of greater than 120 fl. Megaloblastic anaemia typically occurs in the setting of vitamin B_{12} or folate deficiency. Coeliac disease typically affects the proximal part of the small bowel and is often associated with iron deficiency anaemia. Myelofibrosis is often associated with a 'dry tap' bone marrow aspirate, and gives a characteristic abnormal microscopic appearance with reduced cellularity. Phenytoin, as a powerful enzyme inducer, enhances folate metabolism and can cause a megaloblastic anaemia, or less commonly a simple macrocytosis.

157 B: Acute lymphocytic leukaemia

The presence of widespread lymphadenopathy in a young woman is suggestive of an underlying lymphoproliferative disorder, or one of a number of infective disorders, including glandular fever (Epstein–Barr virus (EBV)). However, the grossly elevated WBC makes leukaemia more likely and the presence of lymphoblasts is indicative of acute lymphocytic leukaemia (ALL). The diagnosis is established by histological examination of lymph node biopsy material. Acute myeloid leukaemia (AML) is less likely to be associated with lymphadenopathy. Hodgkin's lymphoma is often associated with lymphadenopathy and hepatosplenomegaly, but is not typically associated with a high WBC.

158   B: Direct activation of factor X

The clinical scenario indicates a bleeding diathesis associated with arterial thrombosis, and the haematological investigations confirm disseminated intravascular coagulation (DIC). Three principal mechanisms underlie the development of DIC:

- Direct factor X or prothrombin activation (snake venoms)
- Direct release of tissue thromboplastins following extensive crush injury or shock
- Vascular endothelial injury (bacterial endotoxins, septic shock, placental abruption).

Treatment of DIC is supportive, and involves administration of fresh frozen plasma and platelets (to replenish and to reduce bleeding diathesis); heparin is of value in certain cases and serves to reduce the risk of arterial and venous thrombosis, and may protect against further vascular endothelial injury.

159   B: Epstein–Barr viral infection

The clinical scenario indicates an isolated thrombocytopenia. The principal recognised causes are:

1.   Marrow disorders (reduced synthesis):
- hypoplastic causes – idiopathic, drug-induced (cytotoxics, immunosuppressants, thiazides)
- infiltration – leukaemia, myeloma, myelofibrosis, carcinoma
- vitamin B_{12} or folate deficiency

2.   Increased consumption of platelets:
- disseminated intravascular coagulation
- idiopathic thrombocytopenic purpura
- viral infections (often antibody-mediated), eg HIV, Epstein–Barr virus
- bacterial sepsis

3.   Hypersplenism: lymphoma, chronic liver disease, tropical infection.

In an apparently healthy individual, with no clinical evidence of liver disease, enlarged spleen, or features of neoplastic disease, the commonest cause of isolated thrombocytopenia is recent viral infection. Bleeding complications are rare until platelet numbers are $< 30 \times 10^9/l$, unless their function is also impaired (eg by aspirin, clopidogrel).

160   A: Lymphadenitis in the right groin
Tender palpable lymph nodes (lymphadenitis) is strongly suggestive of cellulitis, and is the appropriate site of lymphatic drainage of the right calf; occasionally, lymphangitis is observed as redness tracking proximally from the site of the lesion. Pre-existing osteoarthritis is so common that it does not significantly increase the likelihood of ruptured Baker's cyst, although this requires consideration (the latter is more closely associated with pre-existing rheumatoid arthritis affecting the knee on the appropriate side). Pitting oedema and superficial venous dilatation are common features of both infection and underlying DVT.

161   C: Positive anti-intrinsic factor antibody
Addisonian pernicious anaemia (true pernicious anaemia) is a condition characterised by megaloblastic anaemia due to failure of the stomach to secrete intrinsic factor in the absence of an alternative explanation (eg post-gastrectomy). This is the most diagnostic of the features listed, although it is only detected in around half of all patients with pernicious anaemia. Typically, serum vitamin B_{12} values are severely reduced, often < 50 ng/l. Reduced oral vitamin B_{12} absorption may be due to underlying gastrointestinal disease/malabsorption syndromes, although correction after addition of intrinsic factor supports the diagnosis (basis of the Schilling test). Pernicious anaemia is often associated with other autoimmune disorders, including vitiligo and Graves' disease.

162   C: Free haemoglobin in the urine
During haemolysis, normal haemoglobin catabolic pathways may become saturated, and there is often a modest increase in unconjugated bilirubin in the blood; jaundice may be absent or mild. There is increased urobilinogen reabsorption from the gut, which appears in the urine. Haemoglobin liberated into the plasma during intravascular haemolysis is complexed to haptoglobin, which is taken up by the liver and degraded (the haemoglobin-haptoglobin complex is too large to be excreted by the kidneys). In moderate to severe haemolysis, haptoglobin becomes deplete, and free haemoglobin may be lost in the urine. Haemoglobin is partly reabsorbed by the renal tubules, and subsequently degraded to haemosiderin: sloughing of tubular cells results in haemosiderinuria, which is a pathognomonic feature of intravascular haemolysis. Other associated features include macrocytosis (due to reticulocytosis) and, in some cases, a mild leucocytosis due to increased marrow production.

163   E: Penicillin

Methyldopa, penicillin, quinine and quinidine are recognised causes of autoimmune haemolysis. Non-antibody-mediated haemolysis is a recognised feature of lead toxicity. Patients with glucose-6-phosphate dehydrogenase deficiency are more susceptible to drug-induced methaemoglobinaemia and haemolysis; recognised causes are dapsone, primaquine, aspirin and quinolone antibiotics. Interestingly, methyldopa is also a recognised cause of autoimmune hepatitis.

INFECTIOUS AND TROPICAL DISEASES

164 C: Myalgia and raised creatinine phosphokinase are recognised features

The most likely diagnosis is toxic shock syndrome, caused by TSS-1 toxin released by *Staphylococcus aureus*. The treatment of choice is haemodynamic support, and intravenous flucloxacillin. A significant number of patients experience a severe myalgia associated with elevated creatinine phosphokinase (CPK). Although first described in association with tampons of the hyperabsorbent type, toxic shock syndrome can occur in male and non-menstruating females, in association with staphylococcal infection at other sites. Palmar and plantar desquamation is a late feature, typically occurring after one or two weeks.

165 A: High alcohol consumption is a recognised risk factor

The most likely diagnosis is legionnaires' disease, which accounts for up to a quarter of all cases of community-acquired pneumonia. Transmission can be via air-conditioning systems and, therefore, can affect groups of individuals in enclosed environments, such as hotels. Neurological complications, such as cerebellar ataxia and peripheral neuropathy are recognised complications. High alcohol consumption, smoking, male sex and being immunocompromised increase the risk of developing legionnaires' disease. Erythromycin given for three weeks is effective in reducing mortality rates.

166 B: The disease can be prevented using an inactivated toxoid vaccine

The most likely diagnosis is diphtheria. Typically this causes the development of a thick grey membrane over the tonsils and pharynx. Other complications include polyneuritis and bronchopneumonia.

167 B: High-dose penicillin is the treatment of choice

The clinical picture is consistent with acute meningitis due to *Streptococcus pneumoniae*. Meningitis is an infection of the pia mater and arachnoid and can occur as a complication of sinusitis and otitis media. Acute adrenal failure (Waterhouse–Friderichsen syndrome) is a rare complication of meningococcal sepsis. Treatment should be administered immediately, before CSF examination results are available.

168   A: Early administration of vaccine is the treatment of choice
Rabies is a neurotropic rhabdovirus with an animal reservoir in canines and bats. It occurs all over the world but has not been described in Antarctica and Australasia. After infection, the development of symptoms heralds a high mortality rate. The vaccine should be administered early in suspected cases, and is an inactivated whole-cell virus cultured on human diploid cells. Treatment is primarily supportive. The vaccine should be offered as prophylaxis to those involved in animal husbandry in infected areas and to travellers who may be more than 24 hours away from medical treatment if bitten.

169   C: Heterophil antibodies appear in the early stages of the illness
The most likely diagnosis is glandular fever. A blood film will help in establishing the diagnosis, as a blood film from a patient with glandular fever is likely to show lymphocytosis with many atypical lymphocytes, but a normal blood film does not exclude the diagnosis. EBV-specific IgM implies current infection, whereas IgG indicates past exposure. A rash is likely to appear if the patient is given penicillin. Heterophil antibodies form the basis of the Paul–Bunnell test, and appear in the early stages of the illness and disappear after about three months. Prednisolone may be given for severe symptoms or complications.

170   C: The disease is transmitted by the female *Anopheles* mosquito
The most likely diagnosis is malaria. Malaria is caused by a bite from the female *Anopheles* mosquito, which is most active after sunset. The parasite invades erythrocytes, which causes intravascular haemolysis and multisystem organ failure. Prophylaxis is generally required one week before travel (two weeks for mefloquine), and treatment depends on local resistance and sensitivity patterns. Prophylaxis is not completely effective, and does not exclude the possibility of the diagnosis. Malarial parasites predominantly invade erythrocytes.

171   A: Fatality is up to 25%
The most likely diagnosis is Lassa fever. Person-to-person nosocomial infection does occur with index cases having the highest fatality rate. The rodent vector is *Mastomys natalensis* and the mode of spread is via aerosols of its urine. Yellow fever is due to an arbovirus transmitted by the *Aedes* mosquito. Haemorrhagic manifestations are found but these are usually due to coagulation abnormalities rather than thrombocytopenia. Hypotension is often found in conjunction with an initial relative bradycardia. The incubation period for Lassa fever is typically one to three weeks.

172   A: A small rise in transaminases is a common feature
The most likely diagnosis is Weil's disease. It usually follows contact with infected rat's urine. It can cause renal failure, myocarditis and meningitis. It is caused by *Leptospira interrogans*. Canicola fever is caused by *Leptospira canicola*. Benzylpenicillin is the treatment of choice.

173   A: Death can occur from respiratory paralysis
The incubation period is seven days. Polio is a picornavirus which is spread by droplet or via the faecal–oral route. Patients with polio can develop lower motor neurone signs. Fewer than 10% of patients who develop paralysis die, providing there is adequate provision of early ventilatory support and appropriate treatment of secondary infection.

174   D: The condition is caused by a mosquito-borne arbovirus
Japanese B encephalitis is the most likely diagnosis. It is caused by a mosquito-borne *Flavivirus*. Yellow fever is a mosquito-borne arbovirus infection. It may result in encephalitis with a high mortality or residual neurological deficit. South-East Asia, including China and India, are areas at high risk especially following the rainy season. In these areas it is endemic in rural areas but outbreaks can occur in towns as well.

175   E: Weil's disease
Weil's disease usually presents with sudden onset of symptoms, and can manifest with hepatitis, meningitis, renal tubular necrosis and myocarditis. In severe cases, patients can progress to fulminant hepatic failure, acute renal failure, arrhythmia and cardiac failure. Mortality is around 10–20% for patients with liver, kidney or heart involvement. Most patients enter a convalescent phase within four weeks, and make a complete recovery. The diagnosis is established (often retrospectively) from rising titres of specific leptospiral antibody from the second week onwards. Immediate management involves administration of intravenous high-dose penicillin (doxycycline or erythromycin are alternatives in patients who are allergic to penicillin). Weil's disease (leptospirosis) is a spirochaetal infection: the natural hosts for the organism are rodents, and farm and abattoir workers, and those undertaking recreational water sports, are at greatest risk of infection.

176   C: Contaminated water supplies have been implicated in outbreaks
Cryptosporidiosis is caused by a coccidian protozoan (*Cryptosporidium parvum*) and is transmitted by the faecal–oral route. Incubation period is normally seven to ten days, and the infection most commonly presents with crampy abdominal pain associated with diarrhoea. In immunocompetent patients the infection is usually transient and self-limiting. However, in immunocompromised individuals, especially those with advanced HIV infection, the illness can be prolonged, causing severe diarrhoea and weight loss, and pancreatitis, hepatitis and sclerosing cholangitis. There is no established effective treatment, although several drugs have shown promise in early clinical trials. Management involves antiretroviral treatment to achieve a satisfactory CD4 count (typically a count > 180 cells/mm^3 is associated with disease resolution).

RHEUMATOLOGY

177 B: It can be associated with a plantar fibroma in the foot
Dupuytren's contracture is the most likely diagnosis and is commonly found in northern Europeans. It commonly affects the little and ring fingers and is caused by contraction of the palmar fascial bands. It is associated with phenobarbitone, phenytoin and alcohol ingestion but it is unclear whether a true causal relationship exists. Repeated minor trauma is thought more relevant.

178 A: Medication history is highly relevant
The most likely diagnosis is gout, which is due to the deposition of urate crystals in the joints. Monosodium urate crystals are negatively birefringent and their presence is not always associated with pain. Urate deposits (tophi) are commonly found in avascular areas, such as the pinna. Purine-rich foods (oily fish for example) can precipitate an attack, and there is a recognised association between thiazides and, to a lesser extent, low-dose aspirin and the risk of gout (both increase circulating urate concentrations). Men are five times more likely to be affected than women.

179 B: Osteomalacia
Corticosteroids are commonly used in exacerbations of SLE. Osteoporosis rather than osteomalacia is a long-term adverse effect of corticosteroid therapy, the risks of which increase with cumulative drug exposure. Other patients exposed to similar risks are those patients with inflammatory bowel disease and asthma/COPD who require repeated short courses of high-dose corticosteroids. The use of bisphosphonate medication reduces the loss of bone mineral density which is associated with corticosteroids, and appears to reduce fracture risk.

180 E: The dose should normally be 100–300 mg daily, depending on serum urate
Allopurinol is rapidly cleared from the plasma, with a half-life of 2–3 hours. It is metabolised to oxypurinol, which is also effective in inhibiting xanthine oxidase. Probenecid inhibits the transport of organic acids across lipid membranes. Allopurinol can be converted to alloxanthine and this metabolite inhibits the metabolism of the parent drug. side effects are rare. It should not be used in an acute attack of gout but in long-term management to effect clearance of urate from the bloodstream and ultimately the tissues.

181　E:　Recent trauma is a recognised risk factor

The most likely diagnosis is a septic arthritis. Bloodstaining of synovial fluid is commonly due to trauma, bleeding disorders, or septic arthritis. It is commoner in older rather than younger people, although it can present at all ages. Previous or current joint problems and previous septic arthritis are additional risk factors. Less commonly, it occurs after intra-articular corticosteroid injection. It is commonly caused by staphylococcal or streptococcal infections, and antibiotic therapy should be commenced urgently.

182　C:　May present with features resembling lower limb venous thrombosis

The most likely diagnosis is rheumatoid arthritis, which typically presents as a symmetrical polyarthritis affecting the metacarpophalangeal and proximal interphalangeal joints in the hands. The ESR is likely to be raised and there is an association between rheumatoid arthritis and HLA-DRW4. Women are three times as likely to develop rheumatoid arthritis as men. The patient may present with features suggestive of deep vein thrombosis if a popliteal (Baker's) cyst ruptures; this is more common in patients with rheumatoid arthritis than it is in patients with osteoarthritis affecting the knees.

183　C:　It may progress to renal failure and malignant hypertension

Scleroderma is the most likely diagnosis, which is a rheumatological condition typically presenting in the fourth to the sixth decades. Raynaud's phenomenon is an early feature; the gastrointestinal system is often involved and patients may present with dysphagia, heartburn and features of malabsorption. Most patients have a normochromic normocytic anaemia, associated with a raised ESR. Obliterative endarteritis may cause progressive renal failure and malignant hypertension. Vitiligo is a recognised association.

184　A:　Concomitant thoracic nerve compression is a recognised feature

The most likely diagnosis is vertebral collapse secondary to osteoporosis, which may be associated with nerve root compression. Subchondral cysts and sclerosis are typical X-ray findings in advanced osteoarthritis. Nerve deafness and high-output cardiac failure are recognised complications of Paget's disease. Calcitonin acts on bone to reduce the rate of bone resorption and will slow the decline in osteoporosis; bisphosphonates are generally regarded as a more effective treatment, but may not be tolerated due to oesophagitis. Secondary causes of osteoporosis include hyperthyroidism, corticosteroid therapy, long-term heparin use (for example in pregnancy, when warfarin is contraindicated), Cushing's syndrome, renal failure, immobilisation and rheumatoid arthritis.

185　C:　Glomerulonephritis is a common renal complication

The most likely diagnosis is systemic lupus erythematosus (SLE). Although 95% of patients with SLE will possess antinuclear antibodies, they are not specific to SLE. Glomerulonephritis occurs in around half of all patients with SLE. A low complement count occurs in active disease and the neutrophil count is usually normal. Lupus syndromes are recognised adverse effects of hydralazine and isoniazid. These are normally metabolised by acetylation; slow acetylators are more prone to this adverse effect due to higher drug concentrations.

186 B: *Chlamydia trachomatis* is the most commonly identified cause

The aetiology of non-specific urethritis is uncertain. The urethritis is usually sterile, and may be associated with dysuria or be asymptomatic (the latter is particularly true of female patients). There is a very high male-to-female preponderance, around 30:1.

Reiter's disease is a reactive disorder that occurs after non-gonococcal urethritis or enteric infection, and is more common in those patients who are HLA-B27-positive. *Chlamydia trachomatis* is the most commonly identified cause in cases of non-gonococcal urethritis. It is characterised by non-specific urethritis, reactive arthritis and conjunctivitis, and is often associated with an elevated ESR during flare-ups. Iritis is a less common manifestation than conjunctivitis, but can lead to glaucoma and blindness. Other extra-articular features include meningitis, peripheral neuropathy, keratoderma blennorrhagica and pericarditis. Antibiotic treatment is generally ineffective; management consists of non-steroidal anti-inflammatory drugs (NSAIDs) and local corticosteroid injections for relief of arthritic symptoms. Around 10% of patients have evidence of active disease persisting for more than 20 years after presentation.

187 D: Pyoderma gangrenosum

Pyoderma gangrenosum is a non-infective complication of inflammatory disorders such as rheumatoid arthritis and inflammatory bowel disease, and the lower limbs are the commonest site of involvement. There is characteristic deep necrotic ulceration with raised violaceous borders. Vasculitis is less likely in the absence of active rheumatoid disease elsewhere, and tends to cause smaller, discrete ulcers. Erythema nodosum is a recognised complication of rheumatoid arthritis, sarcoidosis, streptococcal infection and inflammatory bowel disease, and typically affects the anterior aspects of the shins; it causes raised lesions with dusky or bruised appearance, but ulceration is not a typical feature. Rheumatoid nodules rarely affect the lower limbs, and ulceration can give a similar appearance to pyoderma gangrenosum.

188 D: Periarticular bony erosions

Osteoarthritis is typically associated with joint space narrowing, which is often more pronounced at the lateral aspect of the knee joint, and is often asymmetrical. Other recognised features are osteophyte formation, and pseudocysts and osteosclerosis of the periarticular bone. Periarticular bony erosion is not a recognised feature and is suggestive of an inflammatory arthritis, such as rheumatoid arthritis. Some soft tissue swelling can be seen in active osteoarthritis or rheumatoid arthritis, although if extensive is suggestive of the latter.

IMMUNOLOGY

189 C: Increased vascular permeability is a recognised feature
The clinical scenario suggests a type I hypersensitivity reaction, which is usually an antibody-mediated phenomenon. Typically, the response is mediated by IgE antibodies that are linked to mast cells and basophils. Cross-linking to antigen stimulates degranulation, releasing a number of inflammatory mediators, including histamine, prostaglandins and leukotrienes. Increased vascular permeability and smooth muscle contraction are recognised features, but the clinical presentation usually involves oedema (may involve predominantly the face, tongue and larynx) and systemic hypotension. The main risk is airway compromise. Immediate management of suspected cases involves administration of corticosteroids, antihistamines and adrenaline (epinephrine), and early consideration of intubation if there are symptoms or signs that suggest laryngeal oedema or other airway involvement. Type IV hypersensitivity reactions are mediated by antigen-specific T cells.

190 E: Selective IgA deficiency
Primary IgA deficiency is inherited in an autosomal dominant or autosomal recessive manner, and occurs in around 1 in 750. A number of other recognised causes are associated with secondary IgA deficiency, including coeliac disease, penicillamine and phenytoin. There is increased prevalence of the HLA-DR3 histocompatibility marker, and around 3% of patients with Still's disease or rheumatoid arthritis have selective IgA deficiency. Most patients appear to compensate and there is increased IgM secretion in saliva and elsewhere. IgA deficiency can be associated with an increased incidence of respiratory tract infections. There is often overgrowth of bacterial bowel flora, causing diarrhoea and malabsorption. In some patients, functional abnormalities of IgG and IgM are found despite apparently normal levels. Patients prone to recurrent infections can be considered for immunoglobulin administration.

191 C: C1 esterase inhibitor deficiency
This is a rare disorder that is inherited or acquired, which can present with recurrent episodes of localised angio-oedema due to uncontrolled activation of C1 and complement cascade. This is usually most evident around the mucous membranes of the mouth and larynx (unlike common urticaria, itch is not a recognised feature). Gastrointestinal symptoms are common, particularly colicky abdominal pain and vomiting due to gut oedema. Acute exacerbations can be associated with hypotension and shock. There is often no obvious precipitating cause, but patients have been known to present after taking non-steroidal anti-inflammatory drugs and aspirin, with a clinical picture suggesting acute anaphylaxis. Treatment involves administration of purified C1 esterase inhibitor or fresh frozen plasma, but is generally reserved for severe exacerbations or for preoperative prophylaxis in patients who experience recurrent episodes.

192   D: Total CD4 count
The HIV virus selectively infects CD4-positive cells, predominantly lymphocytes, but also monocytes, macrocytes and antigen-presenting cells within tissues. Depending on viral load and treatment, up to two billion CD4 cells may be destroyed and replaced daily. When the ability to replenish CD4 cells falls, the CD4 cell numbers become overwhelmed by the virus and the count falls rapidly. The CD4 count is more reliable than the CD4:CD8 ratio, because the CD8 cell count is influenced by concurrent infection and the viral load. Viral load is a useful measure of the effectiveness of drug treatment, but does not provide as good information about the extent to which CD4 cells are able to defend the immune system. Immunoglobulin levels are often elevated, although they may be functionally impaired – often as a result of concurrent infection and due to non-specific lymphocyte synthesis – and autoimmune phenomena are a common feature of HIV infection.

193   A: If both vaccines are required it is best to give them either simultaneously or three weeks apart
BCG and yellow fever are live vaccines and are usually stored at low temperatures. Both are live attenuated vaccines that should not be given within one day and three weeks of each other. There are few strict contraindications to treatment with live vaccines. They should generally not be given for at least three months after receiving immunoglobulin treatment or blood transfusion to avoid the risks of anaphylactoid-type adverse reactions. Live vaccines are avoided in pregnancy.

194   D: Tetanus
Live attenuated vaccines should be avoided in pregnancy and in immunosuppressed patients. Tetanus is an inactivated toxoid vaccine. The other vaccines are live and are associated with a greater risk of complications than in immunocompetent individuals. Other examples of live vaccines include BCG, oral typhoid and rubella.

195   A: Gingival hyperplasia is a recognised side effect
Ciclosporin is an immunosuppressant that acts predominately on helper T cells. It selectively impairs production of lymphokines, particularly the T cell growth factor interleukin-2. It is poorly absorbed following oral administration. Nephrotoxicity is the major drug-specific side effect of ciclosporin, and therapeutic drug monitoring is required to reduce the risk of nephrotoxicity. The daily oral dose in the immediate post-transplant period is usually 10–15 mg/kg and this is gradually reduced to a maintenance dose of 3–5 mg/kg, depending on clinical assessment and blood levels of ciclosporin. Other causes of gingival hyperplasia are phenytoin, nifedipine, pregnancy and acute promyelocytic myeloid leukaemia.

STATISTICS

196 D: There is a linear relationship between the measures

A correlation coefficient (R value) is a measure of the linear relationship between two independent variables. An R value of 1.0 indicates a perfect positive relationship, an R value of −1.0 indicates a perfect inverse relationship, and 0 the absence of a linear relationship. The latter does not imply that the variables are completely unrelated, because a quadratic or logarithmic relationship may be present, rather there is no linear relationship. The P value depends on the correlation found and the number of cases included. Generally, a P value < 0.05 is regarded as statistically significant.

The finding of a linear correlation between age and haemorrhage does not necessarily imply that unselected older patients are more likely to have a haemorrhage than younger ones. This is because of selection bias in the population referred for CT scan where, for example, the diagnosis might be missed more frequently in younger patients or confirmed using other diagnostic modalities.

197 D: It is a measure of the dispersion of the measurements from the mean value

Mean and standard deviation are appropriate statistical measures for normally distributed data (parametric tests). They should not be used to present data that is skewed or has a polymodal distribution, and median ± interquartile ranges are preferred (non-parametric tests). The standard deviation is a measure of dispersal of normally distributed data around the mean, and is calculated as the square root of variance. Standard error of the mean is calculated as the standard deviation divided by the square root of the number of observations ($SD/\sqrt{n}$) and allows comparison of dispersal between two separate data sets. In studies involving high numbers of observations, the standard error of the mean can appear very low and does not truly reflect the dispersal of data and standard deviation is therefore generally preferred.

198 D: The test should identify patients who require further investigation or treatment

It is important to know the natural history of the disease, and an effective treatment for early disease should be available. The test should clearly identify those requiring treatment, and may not necessarily give prognostic information. It should reliably discriminate between those who have a high or low risk of disease. In screening, it is important that the test is reliable in high-risk populations, and it is these patients who should be targeted for screening. The test should be acceptable to the target population, safe and cost-effective.

199 A: Duration of exposure appears to be related to disease risk
In establishing a causal link, there should be an association between the degree
of gas emission and the risk of developing the illness, and a dose-effect
relationship is important. There should be an appropriate temporal relationship
between exposure and illness, and a plausible biological mechanism. Findings
from previous studies are important, as an association should be generally
consistent between studies. Other alternative explanations may exist, for
example tobacco use in this situation.

200 B: It would be prone to bias
Case-control studies are particularly prone to selection and recall bias. They are
particularly well suited to the evaluation of diseases with a long latent period,
but it can be difficult to elucidate a temporal relationship between exposure and
disease. A prospective cohort study is better at elucidating a temporal
relationship, although this usually requires greater subject numbers and a
cohort study is usually more expensive to conduct due to the additional study
follow-up required.

201 D: The trial result is not statistically significant
The analgesic appears to reduce pain more than placebo, and the difference
appears numerically significant, although not statistically significant. The *t*-test
is the most appropriate test in this situation. There is a 30% chance of getting
the observed numerical difference or one more extreme, even if the two
treatments are equally effective. Therefore, the result does not exclude the
possibility of a difference; this is either because there is no actual difference,
or because the study was underpowered to detect a difference. The 95%
confidence interval (CI) is calculated using 1.96 standard errors of the mean
(99% CI uses 2.58 SEM).

DERMATOLOGY

202 E: Lithium
Antipsychotics, antidepressants and anxiolytics all cause a varying degree of lowering of the threshold for epileptic seizures. Lithium is the most likely of the above drugs to have a high risk of lowering seizure threshold and aggravating pre-existing psoriasis. Other drugs associated with provoking a psoriatic rash include β-blockers and antimalarials.

203 D: The Koebner phenomenon is a recognised feature of active disease
Lichen planus is the most likely diagnosis. As well as affecting the mucous membranes, the inner surface of the wrists and legs can be affected. Antihistamines, aqueous cream and topical steroids can be used for treatment, although treatment is often not needed if asymptomatic. Nail damage may occur in about 10% of patients. There is a small potential for malignant change. As in psoriasis, the Koebner phenomenon can be a feature of active disease.

204 B: Clinically the patient may be pyrexial and have local lymphadenopathy
The most likely diagnosis is orf and this is commonly seen in farmworkers who have contact with sheep. It is caused by a pox virus and the patient may present with fever and lymphadenopathy. The red papules that are characteristic of orf usually develop rapidly over a period of one week after infection. The incubation period is around seven to ten days. Spontaneous recovery without treatment can occur although antibiotics may be required if there is a secondary bacterial infection.

205 C: It is caused by a pox virus
The most likely diagnosis is molluscum contagiosum. It is a benign condition and is commonly seen in young children, although occasionally it can occur in adults as well. The lesions do resolve spontaneously although this may take several months; curettage can be used if the lesions need to be removed quickly. Orf is a dermatological condition frequently seen in agricultural workers and is also caused by a pox virus.

206 C: The discomfort is typically worst in fissured areas
The most likely diagnosis is juvenile plantar dermatosis and is commonly found in children aged between 3 and 15 years. Patients will have dry, painful, fissured feet, and typically the medial aspect of the toes is affected (tinea infections classically affect the lateral aspect). Wearing synthetic footwear will usually exacerbate the problem and should be avoided. It is unrelated to allergic dermatitis and allergy testing is usually negative.

MOLECULAR AND GENETIC MEDICINE

207   E: Reduced nitric oxide liberation is a recognised feature of diabetes mellitus

The vascular endothelium is a monocellular lining within blood vessels and the heart, and weighs a total of 2–3 kg in the average adult. In health, it liberates nitric oxide (NO) by the action of NO synthase in the conversion of L-arginine to L-citrulline. NO is a free radical that is rapidly scavenged by antioxidants and haem moieties, and its effects are localised close to the site of release (autocrine or paracrine action). It stimulates relaxation of underlying vascular smooth muscle, causing vasodilatation and increased regional blood flow. NO inhibits platelet aggregation and leukocyte-endothelial adhesion and appears to reduce smooth muscle hyperplasia. Acetylcholine stimulates endothelium-dependent NO activity, while the L-arginine analogue L-NMMA (N^G-monomethyl-L-arginine) inhibits NO synthase; examining the effect of these agents on blood flow responses (eg forearm blood flow responses after intrabrachial administration) allows endothelial function to be assessed *in vivo*. Impaired blood flow responses, so-called endothelial dysfunction, are a characteristic finding in patients with diabetes mellitus, hypertension, hypercholesterolaemia and smokers, and loss of NO bioavailability is believed to be an important early step in the development of atherosclerosis. LDL, especially in oxidised form, is toxic to endothelial cells, causing endothelial dysfunction and allowing LDL to traverse the endothelium and accumulate within the vessel wall.

208   B: Leber's optic atrophy is usually associated with a single point DNA mutation

The Human Genome Project aims to determine the complete human DNA sequence, and to define the functional importance of the estimated 80,000 genes the genome contains. Around three billion nucleotides are found in haploid human DNA, but fewer than 5% of these are believed to contribute to the genetic code. Knowledge of the human genome map is sufficient to map any disorder inherited in a Mendelial pattern, given sufficient numbers of family members. Furthermore, even polygenic disorders such as multiple sclerosis can be analysed. Gene identification has allowed counselling and screening of at-risk individuals, for example for Duchenne muscular dystrophy. A small number of disorders are associated with single DNA point mutations, for example Leber's hereditary optic atrophy and Gaucher's disease. In disorders characterised by non-recurring point mutation, the mutation may occur in any one of thousands of sites within the gene so that screening would be very time-consuming and expensive.

209   E: There is virtually complete genetic penetrance in neurofibromatosis type 1

Neurofibromatosis (NF) is inherited in an autosomal dominant pattern. The incidence of type 1 NF is around 1 in 2500 births, while that of type 2 NF is around 1 in 35, 000. The *NF1* gene responsible for type 1 NF (von Recklinghausen's syndrome) has been mapped to chromosome 17, and encodes the protein neurofibromin. There is complete genetic penetrance of the gene, although there is some variability in the extent to which the gene is expressed and in the clinical manifestations. The *NF2* gene has more recently been mapped to chromosome 22, and encodes a cytoskeletal protein known as schwannomin or merlin. Although type 2 NF is inherited in an autosomal dominant pattern, around 50% of new cases arise through sporadic gene mutation. A characteristic feature of type 2 NF is the presence of bilateral vestibular schwannomas.

210   D: The gene for factor VIII was cloned in 1984

The gene encoding factor VIII is located on the long arm of the X chromosome. The cloning of the factor VIII gene in 1984, and that of factor IX in 1982 has enabled the provision of recombinant factors for treating haemophilias A and B, respectively. A centralised haemophilia A mutation database has been established, and a wide number of underlying genetic defects have been identified. The basic pattern of inheritance of haemophilia A and B is X-linked, rather than autosomal. Carrier females have lower than normal concentrations of factor IX and VIII respectively, which can predispose to excessive bleeding. Rarely, females can manifest with severe bleeding due to inheritance from an affected male and female carrier, Turner's syndrome, or extreme lyonisation (Lyon hypothesis: random inactivation of one of the two X chromosomes in females, so that they are chimeric for X chromosome products, and this may not be balanced).

INDEX

PASTEST BOOKS FOR MRCP PART 1

MRCP 1 Pocket Book Series Second Edition

Book 1:	Cardiology, Haematology, Respiratory	1 901198 84 7
Book 2:	Basic Sciences, Neurology, Psychiatry	1 901198 89 8
Book 3:	Endocrinology, Gastroenterology, Nephrology	1 901198 94 4
Book 4:	Clinical Pharmacology, Infectious Diseases Immunology, Rheumatology	1 901198 98 7

Essential Revision Notes for MRCP: Revised Edition
Philip Kalra 1 901198 59 6
A definitive guide to revision for the MRCP examination that offers 19 chapters of informative material necessary to gain a successful exam result.

MRCP 1 'Best of Five' Multiple Choice Revision Book
Khalid Binymin 1 901198 57 X
This book features subject-based chapters ensuring all topics are fully covered.

MRCP 1 300 Best of Five
Geraint Rees 1 901198 97 9
300 brand new 'Best of Five' questions with excellent clinical scenarios encountered in everyday hospital practice.

Essential Lists for MRCP
Stuart McPherson
1 901198 58 8
The lists contained in this book offer a compilation of clinical, diagnostic, investigative and prognostic features of the symptoms and diseases that cover the whole spectrum of general medicine. It is invaluable for MRCP Part 1 AND Part 2.

MRCP 1 Multiple True/False Revision Book
Philip Kalra 1 901198 95 2
600 multiple true/false questions in subject-based chapters and three 'test yourself' practice exams to give experience of exam fomat.

PASTEST

PasTest has been established since 1972 and is the leading provider of exam-related medical revision course sand books in the UK. The company has a dedicated customer services team to ensure that doctors can easily get up to date information about our products and to ensure that their orders are dealt with efficiently. Our extensive experience means that we are always one step ahead when it comes to knowledge of the current trends and contents of the Royal College exams.

In the last 12 months we have sold over 67,000 books to medical students and qualified doctors. These may be purchased through bookshops, over the telephone or online at our website. All books are reviewed prior to publication to ensure that they mirror the needs of candidates and therefore act as an invaluable aid to exam preparation.

Test yourself online

PasTest Online is a new database that will be launched this year. With more than 1500 Best of Five questions prepared by experts, PasTest Online:
* enables you to test yourself whenever you want
* is accessible whatever time of day
* is reasonably priced and has excellent exam revision tips
* has a choice of mock exam, random questions and specialist questions. This means that you can test yourself in certain weak areas or take a mock exam.

Interested? Try a free demo at www.pastestonline.co.uk

100% Money Back Guarantee

We're sure you will find our study books invaluable, but in the unlikely event that you are not entirely happy, we will give you your money back – guaranteed.

Delivery to your Door

With a busy lifestyle, nobody enjoys walking to the shops for something that may or may not be in stock. Let us take the hassle and deliver direct to your door. We will despach your book within 24 hours of receiving your order. We also offer free delivery on books for medical students to UK addresses.

How to Order:

🖥 **<u>www.pastest.co.uk</u>**

To order books safely and securely online, shop at our website.

☎ **Telephone: +44 (0)1565 752000**

📠 **Fax: +44 (0)1565 650264**

✉ **PasTest Ltd, FREEPOST, Knutsford, WA16 7BR.**